Transfer Pricing: Techniques and Uses

by

Ralph L. Benke, Jr.

University of Georgia

and

James Don Edwards

J.M. Tull Professor of Accounting

University of Georgia

National Association of Accountants

New York, N.Y.

Published by

National Association of Accountants
919 Third Avenue, New York, N. Y. 10022

NAA Publication Number 80118

ISBN 0-86641-012-0

Foreword

The trend toward large decentralized business enterprises has increased the importance of the internal exchange of goods and services among various operations organized as responsibility centers (departments, divisions, subsidiaries). Internal transactions, usually called transfers, may represent a sizable activity for some responsibility centers even where the total volume of transfers is not substantial for the business entity as a whole. In such cases, transfer pricing has an important bearing on the performance evaluation of these responsibility centers. Moreover, if transfer pricing does not reflect the contribution of any individual operation adequately, the organization suffers through faulty allocation of resources and possibly dysfunctional managerial behavior.

Transfer pricing can be seen as a process through which an organization maintains a delicate balance between the overall performance goals and the striving of its component units toward the best possible results within the performance measurement system prevailing in the organization. The pricing techniques tend to have policy implications. It is, therefore, in the interest of the organization to clarify the transfer relationships and analyze the differing impacts of alternative pricing techniques in the light of its overall policies and objectives.

The National Association of Accountants initiated the study, with results presented here in the effort to help business management resolve the complex issues involved in transfer pricing, or, more specifically, to help management accountants provide expert services regarding transfer pricing in their companies. The study findings have confirmed our assumption about the management accountant's role in the selection of pricing techniques. He often serves as an expert catalyst by finding an equitable resolution of divergent segment interests.

The information on current practices was elicited through interviews with the corporate controllers and their staff in 19 U.S. companies from 10 industries with annual sales from $125 million to several billions of dollars. These interviews, along with a literature search, provided the basis for analyzing the advantages and disadvantages of all transfer pricing techniques that have been found in practice or given some attention in theory. One of the interviews led to the general rule for determining transfer prices which is presented in Chapter 5. The concluding chapter (Chapter 6) discusses international transfer pricing and tax considerations.

Guidance in the preparation of this research report was kindly and generously provided by the Project Committee:

Henry M. Klein (Chairman)
Chrysler Huntsville Electronics
Huntsville, Ala.

Carl M. Koontz
ALCOA
Alcoa, Tenn.

Paul E. Dascher
Drexel University
Philadelphia, Pa.

Theodore N. Vaughn
Steelcase, Inc.
Grand Rapids, Mich.

The report reflects the views of the researchers and not necessarily those of the Association, the Committee on Research or the Project Committee.

Stephen Landekich
Research Director
National Association of Accountants

Acknowledgments

The completion of any involved project requires the help and cooperation of many people. This research monograph is no different, but there are several people to whom we are particularly indebted. The first is NAA Research Director Stephen Landekich for his expert guidance from the beginning to the end of the project.

We are also very indebted to Claire Arevalo, Department of English, University of Georgia, for editing the manuscript. Mrs. Arevalo reviewed several drafts of the manuscript and made many valuable contributions. Special thanks go also to Isabel Barnes who did all the typing and still managed to remain cheerful.

Many companies contributed heavily to our effort. All the companies we contacted agreed to participate in our field study even though it meant tying up the time of several of their executives for at least half a day. Without their enthusiastic and candid cooperation, this project could not have been successful.

Finally, we would like to thank Prof. Paul Rubin, Department of Economics, University of Georgia, and our Project Committee, particularly the chairman, Henry Klein, for their assistance and patience.

Ralph L. Benke, Jr.
James Don Edwards
University of Georgia

Table of Contents

Chapter **Page**

Chapter **Page**

Exhibits

Exhibit No.		Page
5-6	Moderately Imperfectly Competitive Markets	89
5-7	External Sales in a Moderately Imperfectly Competitive Market	90
5-8	Two-Tiered Transfer Pricing Technique	91
5-9	Transfer Pricing at the SVC in a Profit Center	93
5-10	The Phantom Market Price as a Transfer Price	95
5-11	The Company Contribution Margin	108
6-1	Tax Minimization	115
6-2	Transfer Prices not Adjusted for Currency Exchange Fluctuations	119
6-3	Transfer Prices Adjusted for Currency Exchange Fluctuations	120
A-1	The Management Control Process and the Transfer Pricing System	137
B-1	Best Joint Level of Output	140
B-2	Perfectly Competitive Market for Intermediate Product	142
B-3	Imperfectly Competitive Markets for the Intermediate and Final Product	143

Chapter 1

Introduction

Business enterprises in the United States face a number of common problems. One common and persistent problem is determining transfer prices: What price should one segment of an organization charge another segment of the organization for a product transferred between them? The segments involved in the transfers can be departments, divisions, or subsidiaries of any size which produce and sell products within the confines of a single country or across national boundaries. All companies of any appreciable size face the task of determining transfer prices because, inevitably, they find it necessary to transfer products between segments.

In order to study the process of establishing transfer prices in detail, the National Association of Accountants (NAA) initiated this study. The purpose of this study is twofold. The first purpose is to examine transfer pricing practices of U.S. corporations (selling domestically and internationally) to determine which transfer pricing techniques are used to establish transfer prices. The second purpose is to suggest a procedure that organizations can use for determining the transfer pricing technique most appropriate for their circumstances. The procedure, covered in Chapter 5, takes the form of a general rule which, if followed, will help organizations select the appropriate technique for establishing transfer prices.

The Importance of Transfer Pricing

Transfer pricing is important for at least three reasons. One reason is that inaccurate transfer prices can hinder the company's effort to earn the highest possible profit. For example, inaccurate transfer prices might encourage managers to make decisions that are in their own best interests but not in the best interest of the company.

Second, transfer pricing can have an impact on segmental (department, division, or subsidiary) performance evaluation. Because a transfer price is the sales price to one segment and the cost to another segment, it is a rare occasion when transfer price does not have some impact on the performance evaluation of either or both the selling and buying segments. Hence, the managers of the segments and all who evaluate their performance rely upon the accuracy of the transfer price. If an inaccurate transfer price sends false signals of performance evaluation, the organization suffers.

Third, transfer pricing is important because of the complexity of the relationships among organizational segments. Transfer pricing between two segments can be relatively simple. Transfer pricing among dozens of segments becomes complex because of the extensive interrelationships of segments. These interrelationships frequently make the issue of transferring products among segments confusing simply because there are so many sellers and buyers, and nearly all are different from each other. An example of the complexity that can surround transfer pricing is shown in Exhibit 1-1, a chart from the records of one of the companies in this study. The chart, referred to by the company as its "spaghetti chart," shows mainly transfer pricing between domestic segments. Equally complex is another spaghetti chart showing transfer pricing between the parent company and foreign affiliates.

On the other hand, some companies would argue that transfer pricing is not an important problem because the amount of internal sales as compared to external sales is low in most organizations; therefore, the impact of transfer pricing is not material. This argument has little merit although, as Robert Mautz's study showed, the ratio of internal sales to external sales is low in most companies.

Robert Mautz, in his study of diversified companies, reported the percent of intra-company sales to total sales of some of the companies in this study.[1] These percentages are shown below.

Percent of Internal Sales to Total Sales	Companies Responding	
	Number	Percent
1-5	249	61.6
6-10	68	16.8
11-15	43	10.6
16-20	17	4.2
21-25	13	3.2
26-30	7	1.8
Over 30	7	1.8
	404	100.0

EXHIBIT 1-1

INTER- AND INTRA- COMPANY PRICING STRUCTURE - I

KEY
STD = Standard Cost
CLF = Cost Level Factor
DN = Dealer Net
U = Units & Attachments
C = Components
P = Parts

ROECO
LIMITED CANADA
JACKSON: SAVANNAH & ATLANTA
TYLER
RAYFIELD
ATLANTA & BIRMINGHAM TRANSMISSION
DETROIT & BATTLE CREEK INDUSTRIAL TRUCK DIVISION
ITD BRANCHES
ST. JOHNS CANADA
CMD ITD
DETROIT
CENTRAL PARTS DIVISION
FUSEFIELD COMPONENT DISTRIBUTION CENTER
BUCAN & ST. ELM
AXLE
ERIE HARBOR AND BENSON
CMD A-W
JOHNS
CIMSA
EUROPEAN SUBS ITD
OTHER FOREIGN SUBS ITD
FOREIGN SUBS LIMA. CM AUSTIN-WESTERN TYLER. AUTOMOTIVE
FOREIGN SUBS MELROE

C=STD+CLF×1.15
U + P = DN − 15%
U = DN: SP = STD + 15%
U OR P = DN
U=N DN−19%: W DN−23%: S DN − 12%:
SP=N DN−16%: W DN−20%: S DN − 9%:
LP = DN − 20%
C = STD + CLF × 1.15
C = STD + CLF × 1.15
U = DN
P = DN
P=STD+CLF×1.15
U = STD + CLF × 1.10
P= STD + CLF × 1.15
P=STD + CLF × 1.05
P=LIST−35%
U =STD+CLF × 1.10
P = STD + CLF × 1.05
C=STD+CLF×1.15
C=STD+CLF
C=STD+CLF
C=STD+CLF
U =STD+CLF × 1.10
C=STD+CLF×1.15
P=STD+CLF× 1.15
C=STD+CLF×1.12
U = CAN DN − 22%
P=CM & AW DN: AUTO=LIST−45%
C=STD+CLF×1.15
P=STD+CLF−DUTY×1.35
P = IT DN − 45%: CM DN − 50%
AW DN − 40%: AUTO DN − 55%
C = STD + CLF × 1.15
C = STD + CLF × 1.15
C = STD + CLF × 1.15
C = STD + CLF × 1.15
U = DN − 10%: P = DN
U = DN − 10%
P = STD + CLF × 1.05 U=DN−10%
P=STD+CLF×1.15
P = STD + CLF × 1.15
P= STD + CLF
C = STD + CLF
C = STD + CLF
U = CM STD + CLF × 1.05
C=STD+CLF×1.15
C=STD+CLF×1.15
U = STD + CLF × 1.15
MODEL 675=STD + CLF × 1.095
U & C = STD + CLF × 1.05
U = STD + CLF × 1.05
P = STD + CLF × 1.166
U = STD + CLF × 1.10
C = STD + CLF × 1.15
P = DN − 45% × 1.06
C = STD + CLF × 1.17
U=STD + CLF × 1.10
P = DN − 45% × 1.06
C = STD + CLF × 1.17
U=STD + CLF × 1.21
U = DN
C = STD + CLF × 1.17
P=CIMSA COST × 1.06
U = STD + CLF × 1.13
P = LIST − 35% × 1.06
C=STD + CLF × 1.17

14 NOV 75

This tabulation, now over 10 years old, shows that for the majority of the companies in Mautz's study, transfer pricing was relatively unimportant compared to external sales. For a few companies, however, transfer pricing was extensive. In the present transfer pricing study, it was found that the majority of companies who knew their ratio of internal sales to total sales reported that the ratio was low.[2] A few companies with extensive vertical integration reported that the ratio of internal sales to external sales was high.

This does not tell the entire story, however. Even in a company with a low percentage of internal sales to total sales, transfer pricing may be very important. The extent of transfer pricing is likely to vary in different segments of the company and, at least in a few instances, be a significant part of the products flowing into or out of some segments. Thus, while the total impact of transfer pricing in the company may be small, it can be significant in some segments of the company.

As a means of assessing the importance of transfer pricing, the interviewees in this study were asked whether they considered transfer pricing important. All responded yes. The majority felt that transfer pricing was very important in their companies; the remainder felt that transfer pricing was only fairly important in their companies. Those interviewees who felt transfer pricing was only fairly important usually cited as the reason a low percentage relationship between internal sales and total sales or general acceptance among managers of the currently used transfer pricing techniques. Nevertheless, all the executives interviewed said that their transfer pricing could be improved.

For the reasons discussed, transfer pricing is important. An extensive amount of information about transfer pricing is available, but the information has tended to confuse the issues involved rather than clarify them. Much has been written about transfer pricing. A wide variety of techniques and methods for transfer pricing have been advanced, but few answers have emerged. This NAA study and other preceding studies are steps toward the ultimate resolution of the transfer pricing problem, but this resolution will not necessarily be the development of a single transfer pricing technique applicable to all companies under all circumstances.

Prior Research on Transfer Pricing

Although transfer pricing has been a problem for quite some time and the subject of a number of articles, little research has been done in this important area. A number of individuals, both academicians and practitioners, have thought about transfer pricing, but few have gotten beyond that stage.

The earliest important study on transfer pricing was sponsored by the National Association of Accountants (then the National Association of Cost Accountants) and published in 1956.[3] This short study, which involved 40 firms, reported some of the reasons why organizations used transfer pricing as well as the procedures and methods used at that time by various organizations.

The only other research study devoted exclusively to transfer pricing was a mail survey of 191 firms conducted by the National Industrial Conference Board.[4] This study, published in 1967, contains a wealth of information on the advantages and disadvantages of many different types of transfer pricing techniques.

Two other important research studies include information on transfer pricing. The first, by David Solomons,[5] was sponsored by the Financial Executives Research Foundation (FERF) and published in 1965. This study focuses on measuring divisional performance and contains a very good discussion on the practical and theoretical aspects of transfer pricing. The second, by Robert Mautz,[6] and also sponsored by the FERF, was published in 1968. This study is concerned with the financial reporting of diversified companies and includes some interesting statistics on transfer pricing.

Research into transfer pricing practices has been sparse. There have been no studies since 1967 involving transfer pricing only, except for a few privately commissioned studies which are not generally available to the public. Our study attempts to fill many of the gaps that exist in transfer pricing research in an effort to understand transfer pricing from a practical and theoretical standpoint, to merge practice and theory, and to provide a general rule for selecting transfer pricing techniques.

The Study Design

Interviews were used to gather information from 19 companies and to explore transfer pricing in-depth. A pilot study showed that constructing an in-depth mail questionnaire on transfer pricing that would not confuse respondents is quite difficult.

The Interview Process

The view of transfer pricing in the present study is primarily a corporate one. Thus, the interviewees usually were the corporate controller and one or more members of his staff. The staff member usually was a controller of a segment or an assistant controller supervising a special department. Some examples of the latter are manager—regulatory reporting, consultant—product cost accounting, director—asset measurement and transfer pricing, and staff operations and systems controller. Thus, those interviewed had firsthand knowledge of their corporate transfer pricing policies, techniques, and problems.

No organization asked to participate in the study refused, and the interviewees were completely open in their discussions. Of all the questions asked, only a few were unanswered, and these because the answer would reveal proprietary information. Some proprietary information was revealed to us under a pledge of nonattribution. In addition, the researchers pledged not to use any information in a way that would identify it with any of the companies interviewed.

With one exception, the interviews were conducted in the corporate offices of the individuals interviewed. Each interview lasted several hours and yielded a wealth of information.

The Sample

The sample in this study consisted of 19 companies in ten different industries, with company sales from $125 million to several billion dollars annually. The companies that participated in the study are listed in Exhibit 1-2.

The criteria used for selecting the sample were relatively straightforward. The researchers felt that as many different industries as possible should be represented in order to view transfer pricing cross-sectionally. It also was felt that whenever possible two companies in each industry should be included in the sample in order to have more than one view. Companies selected to participate in the present study were based on the following criteria:

(1) The company had to have a significant proportion of transfer pricing (at least 5% of total sales); or
(2) The company had to have recently changed transfer pricing techniques; or
(3) The company had to have expressed some concern about transfer pricing.

Highlights of Results

The General Rule

The culmination of the present study has been the development of a general rule for selecting a transfer pricing technique. This rule, discussed in detail in Chapter 5, is as follows:

> The transfer price (TP) should equal the standard variable cost (SVC) plus the contribution margin per unit given up on the outside sale by the company when a segment sells internally. The contribution margin given up is referred to as the lost contribution margin (LCM). Symbolically, the general rule is TP = SVC + LCM.[7]

The application of the general rule depends upon the characteristics of the market faced by the company and the company's management

EXHIBIT 1-2

Companies Participating in Study

Company	Industry
1. Aluminum Company of America (ALCOA)	Metals and Mining
2. Burlington Northern, Inc.	Railroads
3. Caterpillar Tractor	Machinery and Equipment
4. Chrysler Corporation	Automotive
5. Clark Equipment	Machinery and Equipment
6. Exxon Company, USA	Oil
7. Fruehauf Company	Machinery and Equipment
8. General Electric	Electrical Equipment
9. General Mills	Food
10. Honeywell, Inc.	Electrical Equipment
11. Minnesota Mining and Manufacturing (3M)	Chemical
12. National Steel	Steel
13. Pillsbury	Food
14. Sangamo-Western (subsidiary of Schlumberger, Ltd.)	Oil Service
15. Siemens-Allis (jointly owned by Siemens AG and Allis-Chalmers Corporation)	Electrical Equipment
16. Shell Oil Company	Oil
17. Southwire Corporation	Metals and Mining
18. J.M. Tull Company	Steel Service
19. Vulcan Materials Co.	Diversified

control process. Applications of the general rule, which are illustrated extensively in Chapter 5, are summarized below:

Situation	Transfer Pricing Technique
A. Profit Centers	
1. Perfectly competitive market. All products sold internally can be sold externally. (See Chapter 5, pp. 80-82.)	*SVC + LCM = the prevailing market price.*
2. Slightly imperfectly competitive market. All products sold internally can be sold externally. (See Chapter 5, pp. 82-92.)	*SVC + LCM = the adjusted market price*. The adjusted market price is the prevailing market price adjusted for identifiable and quantifiable market imperfections, such as economies fom selling internally. If the market faced by the selling division is more than slightly imperfectly competitive, the adjusted market price cannot be used.
3. Perfectly competitive market or slightly imperfectly competitive market. Most products sold externally. Products sold internally do not have a market price. Production capacity used to produce internally sold products *can* be used to produce externally sold products. (See Chapter 5, pp. 92-96.)	*SVC + LCM = phantom market price*. Since the products sold internally do not have a market price, a phantom market price is created. The phantom market price is the sum of (1) the standard variable cost per unit of the product sold internally and (2) the contribution margin per unit lost by not producing products that can be sold externally.
B. Pseudo-Profit Centers[8]	
1. (A) Most or all products are sold internally	*SVC + LCM = SVC*. This occurs because no contribution margin is lost when products are sold

Situation	Transfer Pricing Technique
and do not have an external price, or (See Chapter 5, pp. 96-100.)	internally; i.e., LCM = zero. The profit center concept can be maintained by using the contribution margin transfer pricing technique.
(B) Most products are sold externally, but production capacity used to produce internally sold products *cannot* be used to produce externally sold products. (See Chapter 5, pp. 96-100.)	
2. Idle capacity (See Chapter 5, pp. 100-101.)	*SVC + LCM = SVC*. Idle capacity in a profit center which would otherwise remain idle represents a zero LCM. The profit center concept is maintained by using the contribution margin transfer pricing technique.
C. Cost Centers	
1. External prices for products produced do not exist or, if they do exist, are unreliable because the market is thin or more than slightly imperfectly competitive. (See Chapter 5, pp. 103-106.)	*SVC + LCM = SVC,* because LCM = zero. However, the buying segment can be charged an allocated portion of the budgeted fixed costs of the selling segment. The budgeted fixed costs are treated as *period costs,* not *product* costs.
2. Idle capacity (See Chapter 5, p. 106.)	*SVC + LCM = SVC,* because LCM = zero. Incremental fixed costs of the selling segment can be charged to the buying segment since these costs are direct if there is only one receiving segment.

Organizational Considerations in Transfer Pricing

The researchers found a surprising degree of interest in this study, even among companies that professed to be very satisfied with their transfer pricing. Almost all of the interviewees could point to weaknesses in their transfer pricing techniques, but many were reluctant to consider a change without good cause. This attitude reflected their awareness that currently no transfer pricing technique fits all situations, and it is often hard to defend one technique against another. The interviewees felt that whatever the weaknesses of their current technique, at least those who used the technique understood it. A frequently cited reason for not wishing to change techniques was the problem of educating those who would be affected.

Many of the controllers felt that they were advisers about transfer pricing rather than policy makers, although one controller of a large segment referred to himself as the czar of transfer pricing. Transfer pricing decisions ordinarily were made by persons outside the controller's office, normally by key operating executives such as division managers. As a result, the technique used frequently reflected some compromise between interested parties, which almost invariably led to a transfer pricing technique that varied from those described in textbooks. The variation was designed to solve a particular problem, reflect a certain circumstance, or conform to a certain objective.

Conflicts involving transfer pricing often were resolved at very high levels within the organization. The greater the dollar value of the product involved, the higher was the level of resolution. Minor problems or problems emanating from low within the organizational structure tended to be resolved by the controller or his staff. Problems, minor or otherwise, that involved large segments and influential key operating executives tended to go first to the controller's office for resolution. If a solution could not be worked out there, the conflict could and sometimes did go as high as the president of the organization. Several controllers reported that in the past their organizations had had some serious confrontations between key operating executives over transfer pricing. All reported that now conflicts are resolved peaceably, even though some executives are not happy about the resolution.

Because it is a technical function, controllers monitor transfer pricing. Within the organization, the controller's staff are seen as experts on transfer pricing, but because transfer pricing affects performance results, important decisions are not made by the controller, but by key operating executives.

Summary

Transfer pricing is an important problem, the magnitude of which varies among organizations. Much has been written about transfer pricing, but very little has been resolved. Confusion surrounds the issues involved and to some extent obscures those issues which are most important.

The present research study was initiated by the National Association of Accountants to examine transfer pricing in U.S. corporations and to make recommendations about transfer pricing. In order to collect information, researchers interviewed the controllers and their staff members from 19 companies representing 10 industries. The results of these interviews are contained in Chapters 2 through 6.

Chapter 2 sets transfer pricing in an organization context. Chapters 3 and 4 describe a number of different transfer pricing techniques and examine the advantages and disadvantages of each. Chapter 5 explains the general rule recommended by this study and illustrates the application of the rule. Chapter 6 discusses international transfer pricing and tax considerations.

Notes

1. Robert D. Mautz, *Financial Reporting by Diversified Companies,* Financial Executives Research Foundation, New York, N.Y., 1968, p. 38.
2. Because of the small sample size in the present study and the tendency of the interviewees to estimate their ratio of internal sales to total sales, the figures quoted during the interviews are not reported lest they assume an unjustified aura of accuracy.
3. National Association of Cost Accountants, *Accounting for Intracompany Transfers,* Research Report No. 30, National Association of Cost Accountants, New York, N.Y., 1956.
4. National Industrial Conference Board, *Interdivisional Transfer Pricing,* Business Policy Study No. 122, National Industrial Conference Board, New York, N.Y., 1967.
5. David Solomons, *Divisional Performance,* Financial Executives Research Foundation, New York, N.Y., 1965.
6. Mautz, *op. cit.*
7. The term "general rule" is borrowed from Charles Horngren, *Cost Accounting: A Managerial Emphasis,* Prentice-Hall, Inc., Englewood Cliffs, N.J., 1977, p. 683. The general rule in this NAA study is similar to one proposed by Horngren, pp. 683-684.
8. Pseudo-profit centers are not really profit centers because the profit is created by the transfer pricing technique.

Chapter 2

The Nature of Transfer Pricing

Organizations that are very different with respect to products and markets may use the same techniques for determining transfer prices, while organizations that are very similar may use entirely different transfer pricing techniques. This diversity occurs because the techniques selected by a company are influenced by a broad and very important company-wide process known as the management control process (MCP). Transfer pricing is a system, consisting of a number of techniques, within the management control process.[1] Unfortunately, there has been a tendency in the past to study transfer pricing without reference to the management control process. This is like trying to study an individual's behavior without reference to his cultural environment. In order to understand the nature of transfer pricing, it is necessary to understand the larger process of which it is a part.

The Management Control Process

The management control process (MCP), which is used for controlling a diversity of activities and elements within the organization, has two major objectives. These objectives are (1) to guide the members of the company toward the company's goals and (2) to evaluate the progress of the company's segments toward these goals.[2] These objectives are illustrated below.

Objectives of the Management Control Process (MCP)

Objective 1: To guide the members of the company toward the organization's goals (Goal Congruence).

Suppose that one goal of a manufacturing company is to minimize the risk of environmental pollution. How does the organization encourage managers to accomplish this goal? Surveys of existing facilities for potential problems can be required. Targets can be set for investments in pollution control equipment. Mandatory educational systems can be established so that managers are aware of potential pollution problems, alternative solutions, and government regulations. In other words, *standards are established.*

Objective 2: To evaluate the progress of the company members toward the goals (Performance Evaluation).

Management needs to determine if the goal of minimizing the risk of environmental pollution is being carried out. Information must be collected. Has the survey of existing facilities been completed? What were the results? Was the survey done well? Are the targets for investments being met? Are managers attending the educational classes? Are the classes successful? In other words, *actual performance is compared to the established standards, and, if necessary, corrective action is taken.*

Because transfer pricing is a system within the MCP, the transfer pricing technique selected by a company must facilitate the objectives of goal congruence and performance evaluation. How can this be done? Before that question can be answered, it is necessary to understand what determines the form of a company's MCP.

The form of the MCP is dictated to a large extent by the structure of the organization. Structure as used here does not refer to the organizational chart but, rather, to the extent of responsibilities of the managers of the segments and to the degree of interdependence of the segments. The extent of responsibilities is related to *decentralization,* while the degree of interdependence is related to *differentiation.* The extent of decentralization and differentiation determine the amount of *integration,* or segmental coordination, within an organization. (Each of these terms will be defined and discussed in order.)

Decentralization

Decentralization, or its opposite, centralization, means different things to different people. There are at least three views of decentralization,[3] and in order to be clear about the view used here, we will discuss all three views briefly. One view is decentralization in a geographical sense. The dispersion of an organization's operations throughout the United States or the world represents a decentralization of activities.

A second view of decentralization refers to functions within an organization. If there is one accounting department, the accounting function is said to be centralized. If each manufacturing facility or division has its own accounting department, the accounting function is said to be decentralized.

The third view, and the view used here, refers to the delegation of authority. The more freedom of action the managers of the segments of the organization have, the greater is the degree of decentralization. Decentralization, however, is a relative term. There is never complete decentralization or complete centralization.

All the participants of this study stated that their organization was highly decentralized with respect to delegation of authority. "Highly decentralized" had different meanings to different people, however, as the following quotations from the interviews will illustrate.

> Company A—Yes, we are highly decentralized. Each manager is free to make decisions as he sees fit. Of course, we are a family-owned organization, so we are close-knit. Mr. .... (the President) is in constant communication with all key managers.

Contrast this view of "highly decentralized" with the following:

> Company B—Each division manager makes his own decisions. He is rarely required to seek the approval of corporate headquarters. We [corporate headquarters] are almost like a holding company. I [Corporate Controller] have little authority over any of the accountants that work in the divisions.

One cannot look at the organizational chart of a business and determine the degree of decentralization within the organization. It would be possible for one organization with five divisions to be highly centralized with respect to the delegation of authority, while another organization with five divisions is highly decentralized. The organizational charts of these two organizations would be similar, but what occurred within each organization would be vastly different.

Decentralization has both advantages and disadvantages, as Exhibit 2-1 illustrates. On the whole, the advantages of decentralization outweigh the disadvantages.[4]

Decentralization has an effect on the MCP objectives of goal congruence and performance evaluation and on the selection of the transfer pricing technique because transfer pricing should facilitate these objectives. As decentralization pushes decision making farther down the hierarchy of a company, it becomes more difficult to coordinate the decisions made by the segments so that they are congruent with the goals of the company. It also becomes more important to measure the extent of goal congruence properly. Thus, decentralization places a heavy burden on transfer pricing.

EXHIBIT 2-1

Advantages and Disadvantages of Decentralization

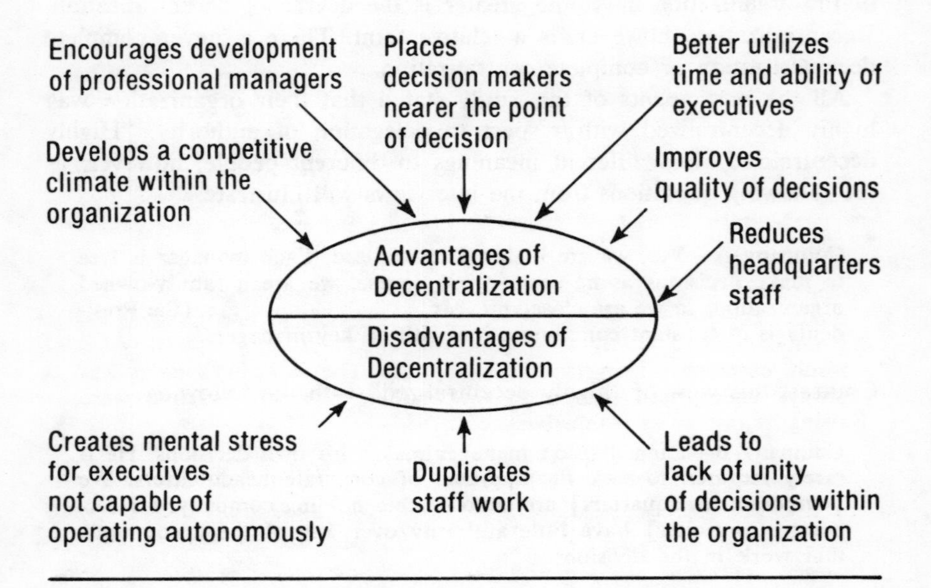

Encourages development of professional managers
Places decision makers nearer the point of decision
Better utilizes time and ability of executives
Develops a competitive climate within the organization
Improves quality of decisions
Reduces headquarters staff
Advantages of Decentralization
Disadvantages of Decentralization
Creates mental stress for executives not capable of operating autonomously
Duplicates staff work
Leads to lack of unity of decisions within the organization

The degree of decentralization, however, is not all that affects the major objectives of the MCP. A second factor is the extent of differentiation.

Differentiation

Dividing the organization into segments causes the various segments to develop different attitudes and behavior, a process known as differentiation. Differentiation occurs because different segments of the organization face different markets, different uncertainties, different work habits, or, in general, different environments.

In organizations with segments that produce different products for different markets, a high degree of differentiation between the segments may be necessary in order for the segments to compete effectively in their markets. On the other hand, if the activities of the segments are closely related, the differentiation necessary may not be extensive. For example, the extent of differentiation in a company with all the divisions selling in the consumer food market need not be as great as the differentiation between a division selling in the consumer food market and a division selling in the home improvement market.

It is important that companies recognize the significance of differentiation among segments. An example of what can happen to a company that fails to recognize differentiation is shown below.

> A very large finance company acquired a paint manufacturing company. The assistant to the controller of the parent company was made president of the paint company. During his first year, he integrated the paint company into the parent finance company and changed the paint company's accounting and financial reporting system extensively to make it compatible with the parent company's accounting system. The results were quickly disastrous. Sales went way up, while profits plunged.
>
> The paint company faced a very different environment from the finance company. The change of accounting systems had reduced the paint company's ability to respond quickly to changes in cost. As a result, costs were rising faster than prices. The company's paint was always underpriced relative to the market, although its costs were rising as fast as its competitors' costs.[5]

In this example the former assistant to the controller failed to recognize that because the environment faced by the paint manufacturing company was vastly different from that faced by the parent finance company, different accounting and financial reporting systems were needed. Furthermore, a different management control process also was needed. If the MCP is different for two segments, it may be necessary to use different transfer pricing techniques in each segment, with both techniques still facing the necessity of supporting the major objectives of the MCP.

Integration

As the degree of decentralization and differentiation increases in a company, the company is faced with the problem of coordinating the activities of the various segments so that collectively they all work toward the company's goals and objectives. This process is frequently referred to as integration,[6] which can be defined more explicitly as "the process of achieving unity of effort among various subsystems [segments] in the accomplishment of the organization's tasks."[7]

Integration is an important problem for companies. The more that segments are decentralized and differentiated, the more difficult it is for the company to coordinate their activities. Ideally, central management will be able to coordinate the activities of the segments in a decentralized company so that synergy occurs. The segments of the company, however, may have difficulty seeing their individual roles in an organizational context. When differences occur, therefore, the segments will tend to act for their own good rather than for that of the company.

Companies use a number of mechanisms to achieve integration, including the following:

Rules, Routines, Standardization
Organizational Hierarchy
Planning
Direct Contact
Liaison Roles
Temporary Committees (task forces or teams)
Integrators (personnel specializing in the role of coordinating intersegment activities)
Integrating Departments (departments of integrators)
Matrix Organization (an organization that is completely committed to joint problem solving and *shared* responsibility).[8]

The list is ordered from the simplest to the most complex integrative mechanisms. As the degrees of decentralization and particularly differentiation increase, the organization is forced to use increasingly more complicated integrative mechanisms.

The application of all of the concepts discussed—decentralization, differentiation, and integration—affect the form of the management control process. The greater the degree of decentralization and differentiation, the greater is the need for integration and an effective MCP. Exhibit 2-2 demonstrates the relationship between these concepts and the organizational structure.

Integrating mechanisms are designed to directly enhance the goal congruence objective of the management control process. A transfer pricing technique that promotes goal congruence is also an integrating mechanism, at least with respect to financial goals.

The Management Control Process and Transfer Pricing

The two major objectives of the MCP, goal congruence and performance evaluation, must be supported by transfer pricing because transfer pricing is a system within the MCP. Another way of saying this is that *the role of transfer pricing in a business enterprise is to promote goal*

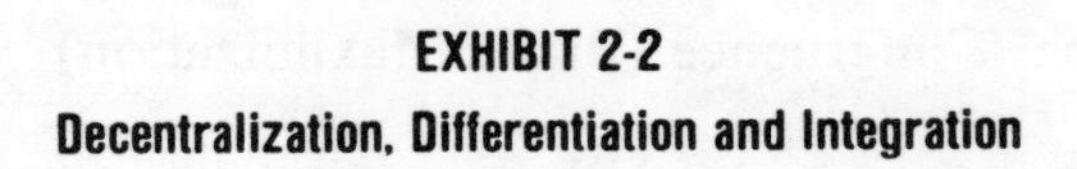

EXHIBIT 2-2

Decentralization, Differentiation and Integration

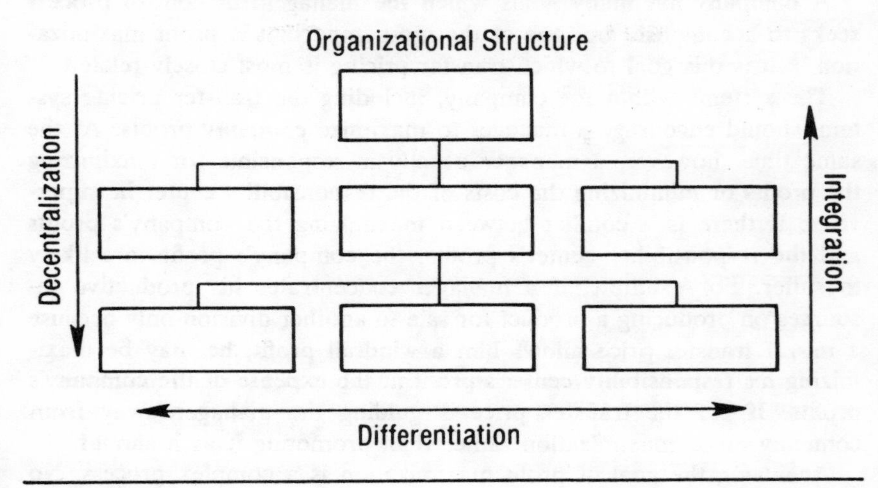

congruence and enhance performance evaluation. How this can occur is shown by the following illustration.

> When gasoline is processed by ABC Oil Company's refinery, coke is created as a by-product. Because the volume of coke sales will be small compared to other major products and because coke has a narrow profit margin, the marketing unit normally would not choose to expend any effort selling the product. In order to encourage the marketing unit to sell the product, ABC Oil Company establishes a price for the transfer of coke from refinery to marketing. A low price will give marketing a large profit margin and make sales attractive. The refineries can, therefore, be assured of an outlet for a product they create in the process of making gasoline. In addition, corporate resources are not invested in large inventories of unsold coke. The transfer price encourages the business units to work together toward a common corporate goal.[9]

For the ABC Oil Company, the transfer price affects both the major objectives of the management control process simultaneously. By establishing a low transfer price, the members of the organization are guided toward an organizational goal, profit maximization. The goal is accomplished by favorably affecting the performance evaluation of the marketing unit. The low price guarantees the marketing unit a large profit margin.

The Role of Transfer Pricing: Goal Congruence (Profit Maximization)

A company has many goals which the management control process seeks to accomplish, but one of the most important is profit maximization.[10] It is this goal to which transfer pricing is most closely related.

The systems within the company, including the transfer pricing system, should encourage a manager to maximize *company* profits. At the same time, however, a manager usually is responsible for maximizing the profits or minimizing the costs of the responsibility center he supervises. If there is a conflict between maximizing the company's profits and the responsibility center's profits, the company's profits are likely to suffer. For example, if a manager concentrates his productive resources on producing a product for sale to another division only because a misset transfer price allows him a windfall profit, he may be maximizing his responsibility center's profit at the expense of the company's profits. If so, the transfer price is guiding the manager away from company profit maximization rather than promoting it as it should.

Achieving the goal of profit maximization is a complex process. No formulas have been developed to show a business enterprise how profit maximization can be achieved or if it has been achieved given the circumstances faced by the business. At best, profit maximization is a rough guide in decision making that may, in the absence of other influential considerations, be an overriding factor.

Because federal and state regulations have increased in recent years, the profit maximization of the early 1900's has been replaced by what might be called neoprofit maximization. Advertising, pollution, employee safety, and many other facets of business life are partially or totally beyond businesses' control. Even profits, if they are deemed excessive, are frowned upon. Although business organizations still must pursue profits for survival, profit maximization is no longer the influential factor it once was in decision making. Profit maximization is subject to many more constraints than in the past, even the recent past. Nevertheless, profit maximization, given the constraints, is still a desirable goal, and transfer pricing must support this goal. An example of how a transfer price can thwart profit maximization is shown in Exhibit 2-3.

The transfer pricing technique selected should avoid situations such as that described in Exhibit 2-3. At the same time it must be remembered that profit maximization is a complex process and is only one goal of the MCP. Other goals, such as increased motivation, may be enhanced by a particular transfer pricing technique even though consistent profit maximization does not occur. Simply showing a few instances where a transfer pricing technique does not lead to profit maximization is not a sufficient justification for not using the technique. Even so, a company cannot stray too far from the goal of profit maximization without suffering serious consequences.

The Role of Transfer Pricing: Performance Evaluation

In addition to promoting goal congruence through profit maximization, transfer pricing also must enhance performance evaluation. Through performance evaluation the company can, in part, determine the extent to which the goal of profit maximization is being achieved. Performance evaluation can take many forms. Examination of returns on investment, residual incomes, and variances from budgeted or standard costs are some of the more common forms of performance evaluation.

The transfer pricing technique should not impede performance evaluation. Specifically, the technique should not allow manipulation or cause distortion of profits or costs of either segment involved in the transfer, thereby creating the illusion of better or worse performance than has actually occurred. For example, suppose that transfers between *profit* centers are made at cost. The center that transfers the product out, the supplying division, makes no profit. The center that receives the product, the receiving division, gets all the profit on the product, assuming it sells the product externally. The profits of the supplying division are understated, while the profits of the receiving division are overstated. The transfer pricing technique, therefore, has impeded performance evaluation. Profit no longer has the same meaning. Return on investment will not be accurate. Comparisons with other divisions within the company may be difficult as will comparisons with similar divisions in other companies.

Transfer pricing is not only important in profit centers, as the example in the previous paragraph demonstrated, but in cost centers as well. Performance evaluation in profit centers, however, is more difficult than in cost centers. Hence, a greater burden is placed on the transfer pricing techniques used with profit centers. Furthermore, the companies in this study used profit centers much more often than cost centers, as is shown in Exhibit 3-1, page 30.

Performance Evaluation in Profit Centers

The performance evaluation of a profit center depends on the differ-

EXHIBIT 2-3

How a Transfer Price Can Thwart Profit Maximization

If a Refining Division sells gasoline to an independent marketer, the division will incur $300,000 in marketing costs. If the Refining Division transfers the gasoline to the Marketing Division, the Marketing Division will spend $2,400,000 on processing and marketing activities [and] then receive $5,800,000 for the 200,000 barrels at the service stations. A selling price to independents has been set at $18 a barrel, while the transfer price to the Marketing Division has been set at $16.

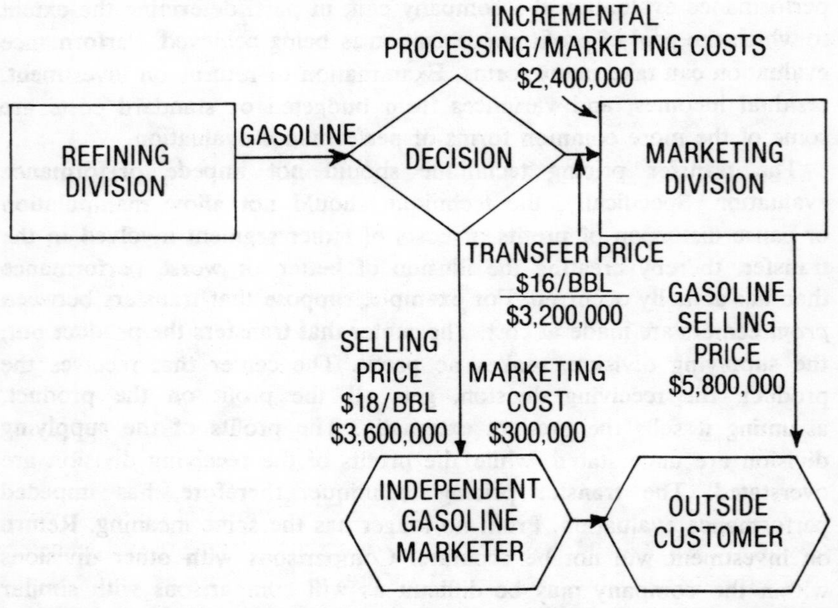

The Refining Division manager would base his decision on the following relevant information:

	Sale to Independent Gasoline Marketer	Transfer to Marketing
Revenues	$3,600,000	$3,200,000
Marketing Costs	300,000	—0—
Profit Contribution	$3,300,000	$3,200,000

Because his division can earn $100,000 more by selling the 200,000 barrels to an independent gasoline marketer, and assuming that the division is evaluated by its level of profits, the Refining Division manager would decide to sell the gasoline to the independent marketer.

An individual who had responsibility for both the Refining and the Marketing Divisions and who used all the information would reach a different conclusion. If the interests of the entire corporation are considered, the alternatives appear different:

	Sale to Independent Gasoline Marketer	Sale to Ultimate Consumer through Marketing Division
Revenues	$3,600,000	$5,800,000
Costs:		
Marketing by Refining Division	300,000	—0—
Processing & Marketing by Marketing Division	—0—	2,400,000
Profit Contribution	$3,300,000	$3,400,000

The corporation as a whole can earn $100,000 more by absorbing the Marketing Division's $2,400,000 in marketing and processing costs, not incurring $300,000 in marketing costs in the Refining Division and selling the product directly to the consumer through company-owned gasoline stations.[11]

ence between revenues and expenses. Because transfers out of a profit center are part of the revenues of the supplying segment and transfers into a profit center are part of the expenses of the receiving segment, the transfer pricing technique selected will affect the profits of both the supplying and receiving segments. The prudent segment manager will seek to transfer in products at as low a cost as possible and transfer out products at as high a price as possible. To the extent that he is successful, the profit of his segment will be affected.

The key to profit centers is making them resemble an independent business to the greatest extent possible. The profit center has both revenues and expenses, its own income statement, and its own profit. Hence, the manager of a profit center must make decisions about inputs and outputs that will affect both revenues and expenses. He will act as if he were managing his own business.

One of the real satisfactions of business leadership is for a manager to see the effect of his decisions on net income and thereby measure his contribution to the company. It is as close to entrepreneurship as a business leader can come, and it can be an exhilarating experience. If the transfer pricing technique used by a company is not appropriate to its profit centers, however, much of the motivational advantage of a profit center will be lost. For example, if a product a manager could sell externally at a profit must be sold internally at cost, the manager may be motivated to avoid producing the product in favor of other less profitable products that are not sold internally.

Even when profit centers are not independent, the motivational impact of entrepeneurship on the managers can be very strong. Therefore, some companies create artificial profit centers by using a transfer pricing technique such as cost plus a markup to create profit. Profit centers created in this manner are not really profit centers, but instead are pseudo-profit centers.

Performance Evaluation in Pseudo-Profit Centers

Because the profit in a pseudo-profit center is determined solely by the transfer pricing technique, the manager of a pseudo-profit center does not have the degree of responsibility that a manager of a profit center has. All a manager of a pseudo-profit center controls is expenses. In this respect, the manager of a pseudo-profit center is no different from the manager of a cost center. Nevertheless, several companies in this study used a transfer pricing technique that resulted in pseudo-profit centers. Consider the following explanation given by the controller of one of the companies interviewed for this study.

> We have a number of manufacturing facilities we treat as profit centers. These facilities are not permitted to sell to other than one of our marketing facilities, so their profit is determined by the extent the transfer price exceeds their cost. We feel this has a number of advantages because the manufacturing facility and the particular marketing facility have a vested interest in the cost of producing the product and its sales price. If the cost of manufacturing is too high, the product may be priced out of the market. If the sales price is set too low, the manufacturing facility may not be able to meet demand or the margin for the marketing facility may become too thin. Transfer prices are negotiated. The manager of each facility has a vested interest in the performance of the other facility. By treating them both as profit centers, we have forced them to work together.

In spite of the controller's enthusiasm for pseudo-profit centers, there is considerable danger in using them when they are treated as real profit centers. When the manager of a pseudo-profit center and his supervisors begin to lose sight of the fact that the center is a pseudo-profit center, decisions may be made as if the center were a profit center. For example, return on investment might be calculated, compared to other profit centers, and form the basis of a decision. Therefore, although a pseudo-profit center may provide some motivational advantages because of the artificial profits, it should be treated more as a cost center than a profit center. The transfer pricing technique should not obscure the emphasis of a pseudo-profit center on cost control.

Performance Evaluation in Cost Centers

A cost center is a responsibility center in which there are only expenses. Whenever an organization uses cost centers, the transfer prices will be based on the cost of the product transferred, although there is not universal agreement as to what constitutes cost. The companies in this study preferred full costing, with standard full cost being more popular than actual full cost.

Some people argue that in a cost center, transfer pricing makes no difference because the transfer price does not affect performance evaluation. According to this argument, once a company decides to use cost centers, none of the other factors that influence the selection of a transfer pricing technique is important. Any cost center transfer pricing technique, such as those shown in Exhibit 3-1, is satisfactory. This argument is not correct, as the following example will show.

Assume that the management decides to use standard costs as the transfer pricing technique to transfer products between Divisions A and B. It appears there is no reason why the manager of either Division A or Division B should be concerned about the actual transfer prices because the managers will be evaluated on their division's deviation of actual cost from some established standard. Products transferred into a division at the cost of the transferring division do not affect the performance evaluation of the receiving division. Similarly, the cost of products transferred out of the division does not affect the performance evaluation of the transferring division (although quantities might). Therefore, cost center transfer prices do not assist in the performance evaluation of either division because transfer prices have no influence on the control of costs. It does not follow, however, that the transfer pricing technique used is immaterial.

If Division B is judged to be responsible for any part of Division A's unfavorable variance, then the transfer price may affect the performance evaluation of either or both divisions. For example, if Division A incurs extraordinary costs to comply with a special request by Division B, such as a change in specifications or delivery schedule, any unfavorable variance that arises as a result of the request is probably not the fault of Division A. Therefore, Division A's performance evaluation may be misleading.

Some companies respond by transferring part or all of the resulting unfavorable variance to Division B, thereby affecting Division B's performance evaluation. Rarely is this a satisfactory solution. Identifying the variance attributable to the special request is difficult. Even if it can be identified, endless arguments will arise over the extent of the variance that should be transferred. For example, Division B can argue that Division A was intentionally careless because Division A knew the variance would be transferred, or that Division A incurred the variance because of inefficiency and that a competitor could have produced the product at a lower cost, or that if Division A were on schedule with other products, a special request to speed up delivery would not have been necessary and no variance would have occurred. Of course, for every argument Division B has, Division A has a counter argument.

Normally, cost centers are used where the extent of vertical integration is high because the volume of transfers between vertically integrated segments is large and the degree of interrelationship between the segments sometimes makes it difficult to assign profit responsibility. Therefore, it will not be often that cost centers are so independent of each other that the performance of one cost center does not affect the performance of another. The transfer pricing technique should assign responsibility to the proper cost center and not allow responsibility to be shifted.

Even if responsibility is properly assigned, however, the argument that in cost centers the transfer pricing technique selected makes little difference is not correct. As shown in Chapters 4 and 5, transfers between cost centers must be at the variable cost in order to promote profit maximization.

Summary

The authors began this chapter by noting that transfer pricing is a system, consisting of a number of techniques, within a very important control process, referred to as the management control process (MCP). The management control process has two major objectives: goal congruence and performance evaluation. The means by which the company accomplishes the two major objectives of the MCP depends upon the degree of decentralization and differentiation and the integrating mechanisms used.

Because transfer pricing is a system within the MCP, any transfer pricing technique used by a company must support the two major objectives of the MCP. Specifically, a transfer pricing technique should promote goal congruence in the form of profit maximization and enhance performance evaluation of responsibility centers. When comparing two techniques, the one that promotes profit maximization most frequently and enhances performance evaluation most completely is more desirable. Thus, profit maximization and goal congruence can be used as criteria for selecting among various transfer pricing techniques.

There are a number of different types of transfer pricing techniques. The major types, most of which were used by the companies in this study, are discussed in detail in Chapters 3 and 4.

Notes

1. This relationship is discussed in detail and illustrated in Appendix A.
2. William H. Newman, Charles E. Summer and E. Kirby Warren, *The Process of Management: Concepts, Behavior, and Practice,* Prentice-Hall, Inc., Englewood Cliffs, N.J., 1972.
3. Fred Luthans, *Organizational Behavior,* McGraw-Hill Book Co., New York, 1973, pp. 136-317.
4. The advantages and disadvantages were developed from James L. Gibson, John M. Ivancevich and James H. Donnelly, Jr., *Organizations: Structure, Process, Behavior,* Business Publications, Inc., Dallas, Tex., 1973, and from E. Dale, *Planning and Developing the Company Organization Structure,* American Management Association, New York, 1952.
5. This example is based on the personal experiences of one of the authors of the present research study.
6. See David J. H. Watson and John V. Baumler, "Transfer Pricing: a Behavioral Context," *Accounting Review,* July 1975, pp. 466-474, for development of the concept of integration in an accounting context. See Paul R. Lawrence and J. W. Lorsch, *Organization and Environment,* Richard D. Irwin, New York, 1967, for the relationship of integration and organization behavior and theory. Watson and Baumler (1975) feel that transfer prices enhance differentiation and play a role in the process of integration. This view is probably correct. Because integration is a part of a much more important process, the management control process, the nature and role of transfer prices in organizations can be better understood through the management control process.
7. Paul R. Lawrence and Jay W. Lorsch, "Differentiation and Integration in Complex Organizations," *Administrative Science Quarterly,* June 1967, p. 4.

8. This list was developed by Watson and Baumler, (see note 6), who in turn adapted it from an article by J. R. Galbraith, "Organization Design: An Information Processing View," in J.W. Lorsch and P.R. Lawrence, eds., *Organizational Planning: Cases and Concepts,* Irwin-Dorsey Limited, Georgetown, Ontario, Canada, 1972.
9. Timothy F. Sutherland, *Measuring Performance Within the Refining and Marketing Segments of the United States Energy Industry: An Appraisal of the Need for Developing Estimates of Functional Profitability,* R. Shriver Associates, Washington, D.C., 1978, p. B-2.
10. Profit maximization refers to achieving the highest possible profit for the circumstances faced by the company. Many factors influence profit maximization, of which transfer pricing is one. Profit maximization is assumed to lead to a higher earnings per share and return on investment.
11. Sutherland, *Op. Cit.,* p. B-5-6.

Chapter 3

Profit Center Transfer Pricing Techniques: Market-Based Prices

There are a number of transfer pricing techniques, each with its own special variations. Although all transfer pricing techniques are related by the common purpose of establishing a transfer price, some are more interrelated than others, thus forming categories or groups of techniques. For purposes of analysis, the transfer pricing techniques are divided into two groups: profit center techniques and cost center techniques. Profit center techniques are discussed in this chapter and in Chapter 4. Cost center techniques are discussed in Chapter 4.

The transfer pricing techniques used by the companies in this study are divided into primary and secondary because the companies or large segments within the companies tended to use a single technique for the majority of their internal sales. Other (secondary) transfer pricing techniques were used whenever the primary one was deemed inappropriate. For example, if a company used the prevailing market price as its primary transfer pricing technique, a secondary technique was necessary for any products which did not have a reliable market price.

As shown in Exhibit 3-1, most of the transfer pricing techniques used by the companies in this study were profit center techniques. Of the 23[1] primary transfer pricing techniques examined in the companies in this study, 19 of them, or 83%, were used with profit centers. Of the 18 secondary transfer pricing techniques examined, 17 were used with profit centers. Only four companies in this study used a cost center transfer pricing technique as their primary one.

The extensive use of profit center techniques attests to the assertion that U.S. businesses are in an era of control and responsibility through profit centers. Profit centers are a natural consequence of a management philosophy of decentralization, a philosophy currently subscribed to by a dominant segment of business managers. Profit centers are seen by many business managers as being up-to-date in business management, while cost centers often are identified with stable, older companies.

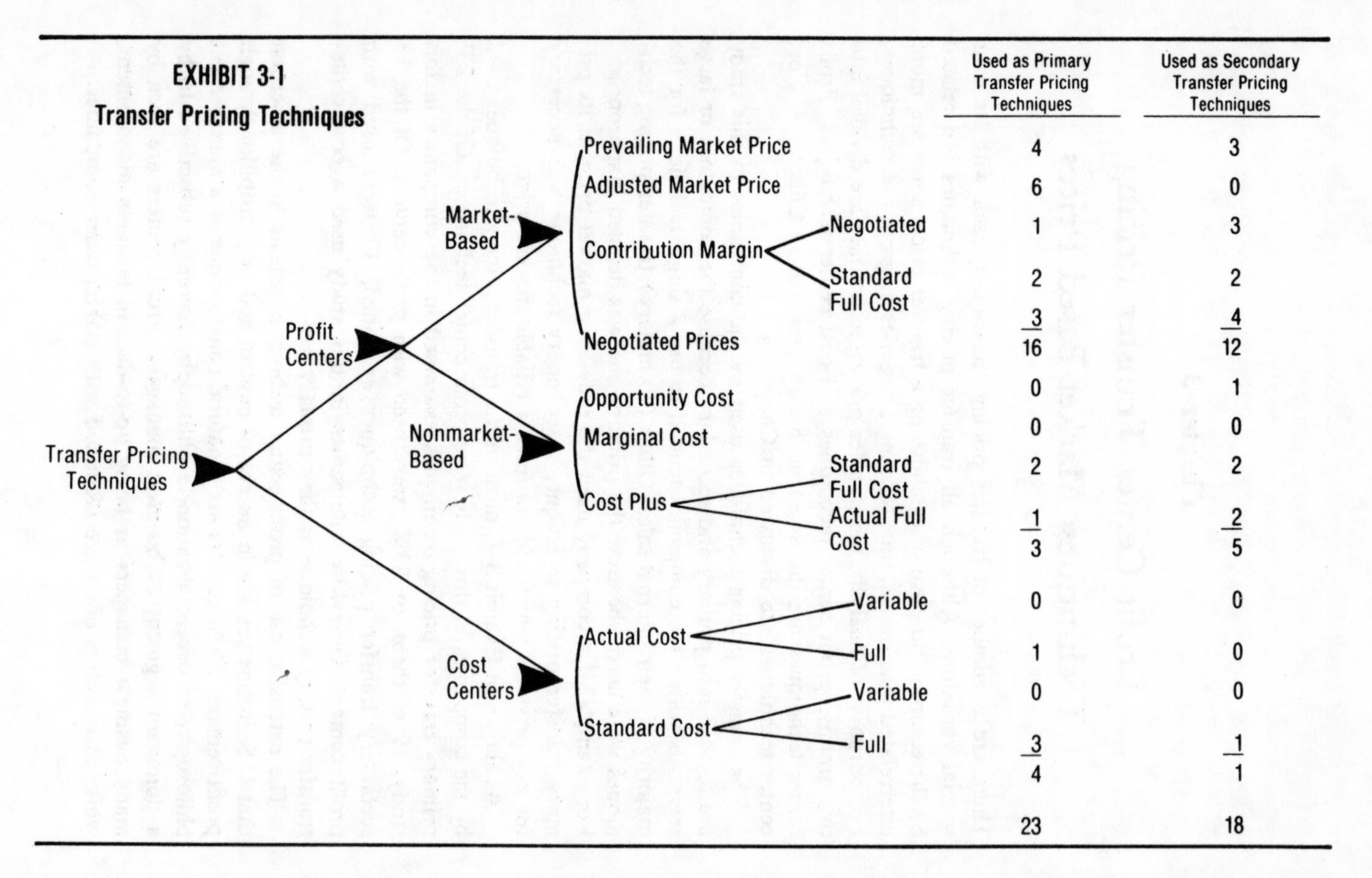
EXHIBIT 3-1
Transfer Pricing Techniques
Transfer Pricing Techniques
Profit Centers
Market-Based
Nonmarket-Based
Cost Centers
Prevailing Market Price
Adjusted Market Price
Contribution Margin
Negotiated
Standard Full Cost
Negotiated Prices
Opportunity Cost
Marginal Cost
Cost Plus
Standard Full Cost
Actual Full Cost
Actual Cost
Variable
Full
Standard Cost
Variable
Full
Used as Primary Transfer Pricing Techniques
4
6
1
2
3
16
0
0
2
1
3
0
1
0
3
4
23
Used as Secondary Transfer Pricing Techniques
3
0
3
2
4
12
1
0
2
2
5
0
0
0
1
1
18

Sweeping generalizations about the users of cost centers and profit centers, however, are not warranted. Sometimes cost centers must be used because there are no alternatives. For example, a company may be so large that market prices are useless because the company would destroy the market if it sold its intermediate products externally, or an intermediate product simply may not have an external price. Nevertheless, transfer pricing techniques associated with profit centers dominate those associated with cost centers, so they deserve considerable attention.

Profit center transfer pricing techniques can be divided into two classes. The major class, which is the focus of this chapter, consists of techniques that are based in some way on market prices (market-based). In this study, 15 companies used a market-based transfer pricing technique as their primary technique, while 12 used a market-based technique as a secondary technique.

The second class of profit center techniques is composed of techniques that are based on cost (nonmarket-based), but which can be used with profit centers. In this study, three companies used a nonmarket-based technique as their primary technique, while four companies used a nonmarket-based technique as a secondary technique. This class of profit center techniques, along with cost center transfer pricing techniques, is discussed in Chapter 4.

There are four market-based transfer pricing techniques: (1) prevailing market price, (2) adjusted market price, (3) negotiated price, and (4) contribution margin (negotiated and standard full cost). All four depend upon the prevailing market price. It could be argued that there is only one market-based transfer price, prevailing market price, and the other three are variations. To some extent this is true. Nevertheless, a more orderly presentation of the salient features of each of the four techniques and their advantages and disadvantages is facilitated by treating them separately while simultaneously noting the interrelationships.

Prevailing Market Price

The prevailing market price is the price at which significant quantities of product are known to have changed hands in arm's-length transactions. The prevailing market price can be a regulated price (in which case significant quantities are less important), a posted price, or a quoted price.

When the market is perfectly competitive, the prevailing market price is an ideal transfer price — ideal because it allows the transfer of intermediate products between divisions while accurately reflecting the performance of the divisions and preserving their autonomy. In a perfectly competitive market, few operating executives complain about the use of the prevailing market price for transfers because the transfer price is the same price they would have to pay if they bought from a competitor.

A perfectly competitive market is one in which any company can purchase or sell a product in arm's-length transactions at the prevailing market price. In other words, the price is firm. A company can plan to buy or sell all it wishes, confident that it will be able to do so at the prevailing market price. An example of a perfectly competitive market is the crude oil market. All crude oil produced can be sold at the prevailing (regulated) market price.

Sometimes whether a market for a particular company is perfectly competitive depends upon the size of the company. For example, in a market with one dominant company and numerous small ones, a small aluminum company probably can sell all the aluminum ingots it can produce at the prevailing market price. For that company, because of the dominant price leadership of other companies, the market is perfectly competitive. On the other hand, the market is not perfectly competitive for a larger, dominant aluminum company. If a large aluminum company attempted to sell any significant quantity of its aluminum ingots externally, the bottom would drop right out of the market.

Unfortunately, few firms can either buy or sell in a perfectly competitive market. The much more frequent situation is that the market is imperfectly competitive. What makes a market imperfectly competitive? David Solomons, in his book, *Division Performance: Measurement and Control,* described an imperfectly competitive market very well:

> Several factors conspire to create this situation [imperfectly competitive markets]. The transferred product may have special characteristics which differentiate it from other varieties of what may loosely be termed the "same" product. As a result, the market for it may, in fact, be quite restricted. This means that the ruling [prevailing] price will not be independent of the activities of the two divisions. In particular, it is likely to be sensitive to any quantities which the supplying division sells on the market or which the consuming division buys on the market. In the limit, of course, where the transferred product is really unique in important respects, it can no longer be said to have a "market" at all. Well short of this point, however, a so-called market price may be so hedged with qualifications that it may have no immediate validity for transfer pricing purposes. There may be discounts for particular types of trades or for different conditions of sale. A given price may mean many different things according to the terms relating to delivery, payment, service and warranty which constitute part of the deal. Posted prices may not have the significance they appear to have if transactions are infrequent. The price for a given commodity may be widely different in a long-term contract from

> what it would be in an isolated transaction. The price obtainable by a seller may be very different from the price payable by a buyer when selling expenses and other costs of finding a customer are taken into account.
>
> All these complications are symptoms of a single condition—the market for the transferred product is not perfectly competitive. In a perfectly competitive market there would be one price for the product —and that price would not be sensitive to the quantities bought or sold by the divisions of a single company. There would be uniform conditions of sale, and selling expenses would be unimportant, if not completely absent.[2]

As Solomons' comments clearly indicate, few companies face a perfectly competitive market. It is not really necessary, however, for a market to be perfectly competitive in order to provide a useful transfer price. Modest amounts of imperfection can be tolerated with only a small loss of efficiency. Many companies, except for perhaps the dominating ones or those facing narrow markets, face slightly imperfectly competitive markets. That is, these companies could sell all the product they transfer internally to external customers, but in order to do so, some price concession or special condition would be necessary.

On the other hand, some companies obviously cannot sell any significant portion of their internal transfers to external customers without substantial price concessions. These companies would saturate the market before all their internal transfers were sold externally, either because of the high volume of internal sales or because of a small market for the product.

If the market imperfections are minor, the problems involved in using the prevailing market price are small, and it can be used for internal transfers of intermediate products. If the market imperfections are major, the prevailing market price clearly cannot be used. But these are two extremes. What of the companies that fall between the extremes?

Companies that have markets with imperfections between these two extremes probably cannot use the prevailing market price as a transfer price and may have to use pseudo-profit centers or, more preferably, cost centers. The prevailing market price cannot be used because there is a series of market prices, depending upon the volume sold externally. For example, a company might face the demand schedule shown on page 34.

The demand schedule shows that the sales price per unit depends on the number of units sold externally. The more units sold externally in an imperfectly competitive market, the lower the sale price per unit must be to entice buyers. Suppose that a company currently sells 2,000 units externally and 3,000 units internally. The prevailing market price

Unit Sales	Sales Price Per Unit	Total Revenue	(Increase)
1,000	20	20,000	
2,000	18	36,000	16,000
3,000	16	48,000	12,000
4,000	14	56,000	8,000
5,000	12	60,000	4,000

for the 2,000 units, according to the demand schedule, would be $18 per unit. If this price is used as the transfer price, the supplying division will have revenue of $90,000 [(2,000) ($18) + 3,000 ($18)].

What happens, however, if the receiving division decides not to buy and discontinues using the product produced by Division A? When the 3,000 units previously sold internally are sold externally, the price for each of the 5,000 units drops to $12 per unit, generating $60,000 in revenue, a decline of $30,000 for the supplying division. The transfer price of $18 per unit for the 3,000 units sold internally implicitly assumed that these units could be sold externally for $18 per unit, when, in fact, they could not. Assuming that the internal sales could be sold at external prices clearly is unrealistic and would lead to non-profit-maximizing decisions. What then should the transfer price be? The answer is complicated.

If left to the supplying and receiving divisions to determine, the transfer price will depend upon the extent to which the receiving division can exercise monopolistic control over the supplying division. If the supplying division cannot sell the amount of product it wants to anyone other than the receiving division without substantial price concession, the receiving division can drive the price down for internal sales to well below the prevailing market price. Conversely, if the receiving division must have the product and cannot buy the amount of product it wants from anyone other than the supplying division, the supplying division has little incentive to lower the price below the prevailing market price for internal sales to the receiving division even though the supplying division could not sell the transferred products externally at the prevailing market price. Lesser degrees of monopolistic control by the supplying division will lead to lower transfer prices, but it is unlikely that the transfer price will be established at a level that allows the company to maximize its profits.

Profit maximization can be achieved by examining the profit opportunities and respective costs of both divisions simultaneously to determine the appropriate level of external and internal sales; a two-tiered transfer price then is established. For example, when the supplying division is a monopoly, external sales are at the prevailing market price, which allows the supplying division to exploit whatever monopolistic power it has over external customers. Internal sales are at the marginal cost of the supplying division. The transfer price is dictated to the supplying division, as is the output level, to avoid any monopolistic control by the supplying division over the receiving division.

Although a dictated, two-tiered pricing system achieves profit maximization, it has a number of severe problems. First, there is a considerable loss of divisional autonomy. This may or may not be tolerable. Second, there is the difficult problem of determining the marginal cost of the supplying division. Third, the supplying division will be a profit center with respect to external sales but a cost center for internal sales, which makes performance evaluation difficult. Thus, a two-tiered pricing system such as the one described above holds little promise in an imperfectly competitive market.

In summary, when the prevailing market price is a feasible transfer price, its advantages are significant. For one thing, it facilitates performance measurement because it is the same price that the buying division would pay if it purchased externally. Furthermore, the autonomy of the divisions is preserved. Each division can act as an independent unit.

Opportunities for using the prevailing market price as the transfer price are rare, however, because the basic requirement for the use of the prevailing market price, perfectly competitive markets, is likely to be absent. If the market imperfections are slight, the prevailing market price can still be used at small loss of efficiency. If the market imperfections are anything other than slight, however, the prevailing market price should not be used. A special two-tiered dictated transfer pricing technique can be used, but this technique poses difficult problems. Alternatively, the divisions can be converted to cost centers which in turn can be reinstated as pseudo-profit centers through the use of the contribution margin approach.

Adjusted Market Price

The adjusted market price was the most popular transfer price among the companies in this study. The adjusted market price is simply the prevailing market price adjusted for market imperfections that are avoided by selling internally. For example, the supplying division will not incur any significant selling expenses or bad debt expense if it sells internally. Therefore, in order to motivate the receiving division to buy internally, the prevailing market price is adjusted downward by the amount of cost the supplying division avoids by selling internally. Most of the companies in this study encouraged internal buying, and this policy often was reflected in the adjusted market price. Two companies, however, had strict market price policies — no discounts for internal sales. Each division had to stand strictly on its own. This difference represents a difference in the extent of decentralization within the companies, the greater decentralization being within the companies that used strict market prices.

Economies other than selling expenses and bad debt also may occur. One company deducted two percent for investment not tied up in accounts receivable. Another company deducted transportation expenses not incurred for certain internal sales. A third company made no effort to determine the actual savings; it simply deducted a standard percentage of five percent from the prevailing market price.

The advantage of the adjusted market price is that it encourages internal sales. Many companies felt that if the intermediate products made by their companies were worthwhile, they should be used. Some felt that buying internally, assuming the adjusted market price was fair, promoted goodwill among various segments of the organization.

The adjusted market price, however, is subject to the same important disadvantage as the prevailing market price. That is, the adjusted market price, because it is a variation of the prevailing market price, is useful only in perfectly competitive or nearly perfectly competitive markets.

In addition, there are two minor disadvantages to the adjusted market price. The receiving and supplying division may not always agree on what a fair adjustment is because the amount of the savings is sometimes difficult to determine. A second problem is that comparison of the receiving division's profitability with that of other companies can be slightly obscured because of the variable buying price of the division.

Negotiated Prices

To a large extent, negotiated prices, as a transfer pricing technique, are very similar to adjusted market prices so have many of the attendant advantages and disadvantages. They are similar because in almost all instances the negotiation takes place around the prevailing market price. Thus, the discount for internal sales is being negotiated, which in essence is the adjusted market price. This was the case with the three companies that used negotiated transfer prices as their primary transfer pricing technique. For all three companies, the prevailing market price formed the upper boundary in the negotiated price.

For the five companies that used negotiated prices as their secondary transfer pricing technique, the negotiation by four of them was not necessarily around the prevailing market price. One company allowed negotiation around the prevailing market price for similar products. Another company allowed negotiations around competitors' prices, but only when the buying division faced a competitive situation. Two companies allowed unrestricted negotiations whenever the adjusted market price, which was their primary transfer pricing technique, could not be used.

The companies in this study had varying experiences with negotiated prices. Two companies said that in order to promote autonomy between divisions, their primary transfer pricing technique at one time had been unrestricted negotiations. Serious conflicts between divisional managers occurred, however, and quite often these conflicts had to be resolved by the president of the company. One of the two companies changed to cost centers because they were more consistent with the vertical integration in the company. The second company began dictating transfer prices somewhat arbitrarily in order to reduce the conflict between divisional managers.

Much acclaim has been made about the advantages a manager skilled in negotiations can gain over a less-skilled manager. One company, which previously had used unrestricted negotiation, found that some managers spent considerable time analyzing external market conditions for the products they purchased internally and became skilled negotiators as a result. Several managers negotiated highly favorable transfer prices that significantly improved the profitability of their division. Most of this skilled negotiation occurred, however, with products that did not have firm market prices. In other words, the markets for the transferred products were from moderately to significantly imperfectly competitive.

The companies that used negotiated prices as their primary transfer pricing technique professed to have few difficulties with negotiations because the negotiation was around a fairly firm market price. The most that could be negotiated was adjustments for economies from selling internally, so there was little opportunity for a skilled negotiator to gain an advantage.

The companies using negotiated prices as their secondary transfer pricing technique professed to have few problems even though the range of negotiation was wider because the market was narrower and market prices seldom were either reliable or firm. The companies felt that the volume of transfers negotiated under these circumstances was too small to generate any important problems.

If a company's purpose in using negotiations is to allow the managers of the receiving and supplying divisions to negotiate economies from selling internally, it probably is better to establish company policies on the economies. That is, the company should specify what economies — for example, bad debt expense avoided or selling expenses not incurred — are to be deducted from the prevailing market price. Such policies will avoid misunderstandings and reduce the possibility of either the receiver or supplier taking advantage of a monopoly position. If the company has a "buy internal" policy, the supplier has a significant advantage over the receiver in a negotiation process if there are no company policies to guide the negotiation.

Contribution Margin

The contribution margin transfer pricing technique involves allocating the contribution margin (sales price minus all variable costs) between the supplying division and the receiving division. For example, assume that a product with a sales price of $20 has variable costs of $11, giving a contribution margin of $9. Further, assume that the variable cost of $11 is divided $8-$3 between the supplying and receiving divisions respectively. Using the variable costs each incurred as a basis, the contribution margin can be allocated between the supplying and receiving divisions. If so, the analysis would be as shown in Exhibit 3-2.

To determine the transfer price for Division A's product, the contribution margin per unit of the final product for the company first must be determined. In Exhibit 3-2, the contribution margin is $9. The $9 is then divided between Divisions A and B, based on their respective variable costs. The contribution margin allocated to Division A is $6.55, so the transfer price for Division A is $14.55 [$6.55 + $8.00(VC)]. Both divisions will be pseudo-profit centers because the profit of each division depends upon the allocation process. Whether the divisions actually have a profit, however, depends on whether the contribution margin per unit allocated to each division multiplied by the volume exceeds fixed costs.

In essence, the contribution margin technique is a value-added approach to transfer pricing.[8] Each division receives a percentage of the company's total contribution that, in the example, is based on the variable cost. Any other basis could be used, and in Chapter 5 it is argued that standard variable cost rather than variable cost is a preferable basis. Any number of divisions can be involved in this process, with the transfer price of each equal to the transferred-in price plus variable costs plus the contribution margin allocated to that division.

EXHIBIT 3-2
Contribution Margin Transfer Pricing Technique

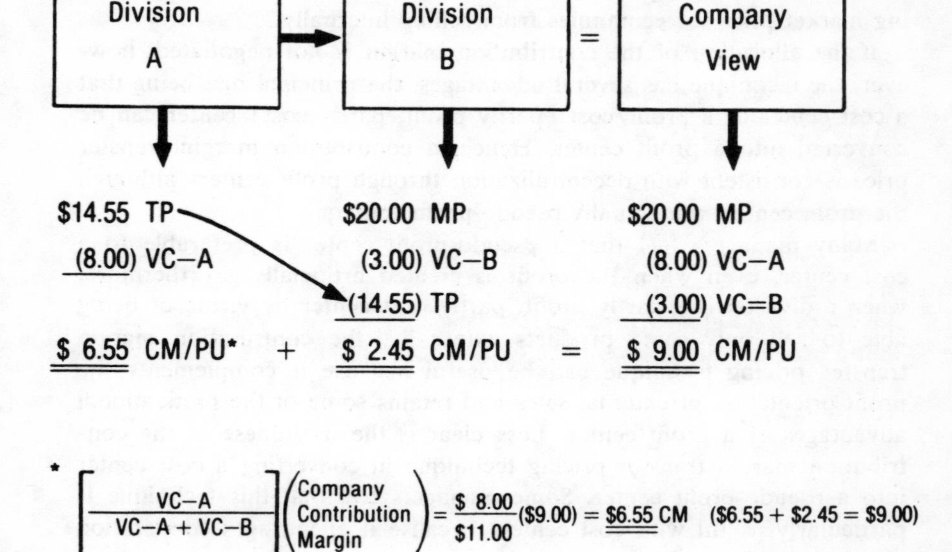

TP = Transfer price VC—A = Variable cost of Division A

MP = Market price VC—B = Variable cost of Division B

CM/PU = Contribution margin per unit

A surprising number of companies in this study used the contribution margin technique. Three companies used it as their primary transfer pricing technique, while four used it as a secondary technique. Four of these companies allowed the division to negotiate the allocation of the contribution margin, but this negotiation of the allocation is undesirable for two reasons.

First, negotiation of the contribution margin may cause the company to suboptimize profit by missing profitable opportunities. If one of the two managers involved in the negotiation feels he is not receiving his fair share of the contribution margin, he may refuse to participate. If so, the company will be the loser unless other, more profitable alternatives are developed.

Second, the negotiation process is likely to be time consuming and may cause conflicts. Each manager will seek the largest possible share of the contribution margin, and the most skillful negotiator can gain important advantages for his division. Negotiation can work well only when the amount being negotiated is contained in a small range, as it would be if the managers were negotiating deductions from the prevailing market price for economies from selling internally.

If the allocation of the contribution margin is not negotiated, however, the technique has several advantages, the principal one being that a cost center or a profit/cost (partly profit, partly cost) center can be converted into a profit center. Hence, a contribution margin transfer price is consistent with decentralization through profit centers although the profit centers are actually pseudo-profit centers.

Many managers feel that a pseudo-profit center is preferable to a cost center, even when the profit is created artificially. Furthermore, when a division is a partly profit, partly cost center by virtue of being able to sell only some products externally, the contribution margin transfer pricing technique can be useful because it complements the profit orientation of external sales and retains some of the motivational advantages of a profit center. Less clear is the usefulness of the contribution margin transfer pricing technique in converting a cost center into a pseudo-profit center. Some managers feel that this technique is particularly useful with cost centers because it encourages cooperation between divisions.

The second advantage of the contribution margin technique is that it encourages divisions to act together since the ultimate profit of each is dependent upon the contribution margin received by the company. Division B will be very interested in Division A's cost performance because the transfer price and company profit improve with cost efficiency. Any assistance Division B can render Division A that leads to cost savings, such as avoiding rush orders, will benefit both divisions. On the other hand, Division A has a vested interest in Division B's ability to sell the product at the prevailing market price. Any assistance it can render Division B in advancing sales, such as conducting a mini-course in production for the sales force, will benefit both divisions. In essence, Division A and Division B form a single profit center with respect to the products involved, with both divisions being treated as pseudo-profit centers for any products transferred using a contribution margin transfer price.

Unfortunately, the cooperation promoted by a contribution margin transfer pricing technique is also something of a disadvantage because a division that finds a means of reducing its costs does not receive the entire benefit of the cost reduction. It must be shared with the other division in proportion to the split of the contribution margin. Suppose, for example, that Division A, as shown in Exhibit 3-2, is able to reduce its variable costs by 10% to $7.20. The analysis is shown in Exhibit 3-3.

EXHIBIT 3-3
Cost Reduction in Division A

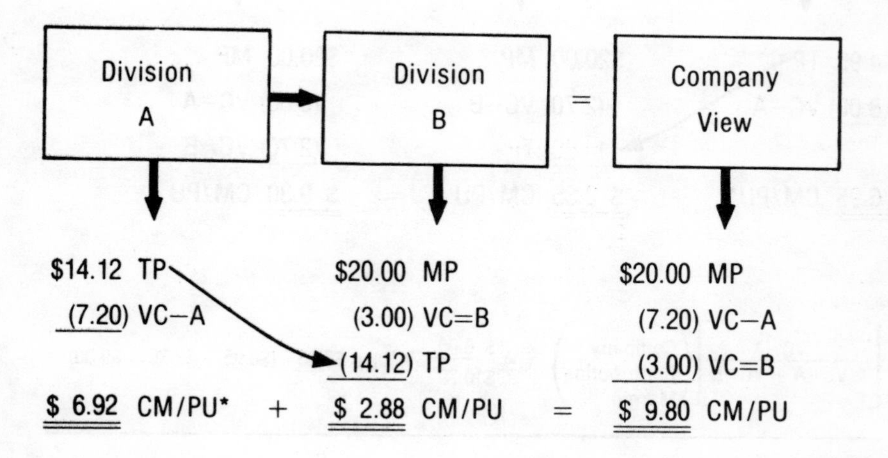

$$^{*}\left[\frac{\text{VC—A}}{\text{VC—A} + \text{VC—B}}\right]\left(\begin{array}{l}\text{Company}\\ \text{Contribution}\\ \text{Margin}\end{array}\right) = \frac{\$\,7.20}{\$10.20}(\$9.80) = \$6.92 \quad (\$6.92 + \$2.88 = \$9.80)$$

The contribution margin for the company is now $9.80, reflecting the decrease in Division A's variable cost. Of the $.80 decrease in variable cost, however, Division A retains only $.37, ($6.92 − $6.55), while Division B receives $.43, ($2.88 − $2.45). In other words, Division A generates all of the $.80 increase in the company's contribution margin but retains only 46.25% of the increase.

A cost reduction of 10% in Division B has an even worse effect, as shown in Exhibit 3-4. The $.30 increase in the company's contribution margin per unit is caused by the 10% reduction in Division B's

EXHIBIT 3-4

Cost Reduction in Division B

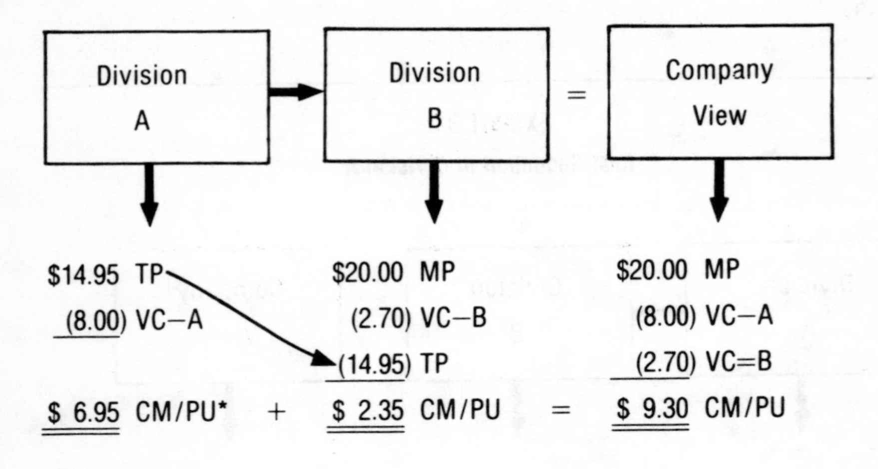

$$^{*}\left[\frac{\text{VC–A}}{\text{VC–A} + \text{VC–B}}\right]\left(\begin{array}{l}\text{Company}\\ \text{Contribution}\\ \text{Margin}\end{array}\right) = \frac{\$\ 8.00}{\$10.70}(\$9.30) = \underline{\underline{\$6.95}} \quad (\$6.95 + \$2.35 = \$9.30)$$

variable cost. Division B's contribution margin per unit after initiating the cost savings is $2.35, which is $.10 per unit lower than it was before initiating the cost savings, or $2.45 in Exhibit 3-2 as compared to $2.35 in Exhibit 3-4. In fact, Division B actually could increase its contribution margin per unit by increasing its variable cost. The company's contribution margin per unit would go down, while Division B's contribution margin per unit would go up. The real loser is Division A because even though its costs do not change, its contribution margin per unit will decline.

The results shown in Exhibit 3-4 are caused by the imbalance in the ratio of variable costs, $8 versus $3, between Division A and Division B. As the variable costs become closer to being equal, results such as those described in the previous paragraph will not occur. Nevertheless, it is characteristic of a contribution margin transfer pricing technique that cost savings as well as cost increases must be shared.

The split of the contribution margin need not be based on cost, either actual or standard, but when a basis other than cost is used, arguments about the relative contribution of each division will occur. Negotiation between the two divisions on the allocation of the cost savings also will create arguments because the manager of the division achieving the cost savings can argue effectively that he should retain all the savings. However, if Division A retains all the cost savings it generates, Division B loses its incentive to cooperate with Division A on cost savings.

All of this leads to the second disadvantage of the contribution margin transfer price, which is that it becomes easy to forget that Division A and Division B are, in essence, a single profit center with respect to the products transferred. Arguments over the allocation of changes in the contribution margin clearly are dysfunctional. Nothing can be gained, and something can be lost because the only important consequence is what happens to the company's contribution margin. Thus, if this transfer pricing technique is used, it should be used with some caution, no matter what the basis of the allocation of the contribution margin. Top management should view Division A and Division B as a single profit center for control and resource allocation purposes, using cost control primarily as the means of measuring the performance evaluation of any pseudo-profit center, such as the divisions in the above example.

A Concern about Market-Based Transfer Pricing Techniques

Three companies in this study expressed concern about the effect of profit buildup on their product decisions. Profit buildup occurs when a product is transferred through several profit centers: each transferring center adds a profit. The controllers of the three companies felt that profit buildup squeezes the profit of the final profit center, which may make nonprofit maximizing decisions.

Exhibit 3-5, which shows the flow of the Mideast division of a company in this study, demonstrates how the profit buildup can occur. Stone Products transfers part of its stone to Hot-Mix Products at the prevailing market price. Hot-Mix Products processes the stone and transfers part of it at the prevailing market price to Wesco Construction, who, in turn, sells the product externally. All of these companies report to the Mideast division manager.

By the time the product reaches Wesco Construction, the normal profit from Stone Products sales and Hot-Mix Products sales is included in the market price. If Wesco Construction accepts the transfer price as its cost of sales, it may decide not to make external sales of the

EXHIBIT 3-5

Profit Buildup with Market-Based Transfer Pricing

Mideast Division

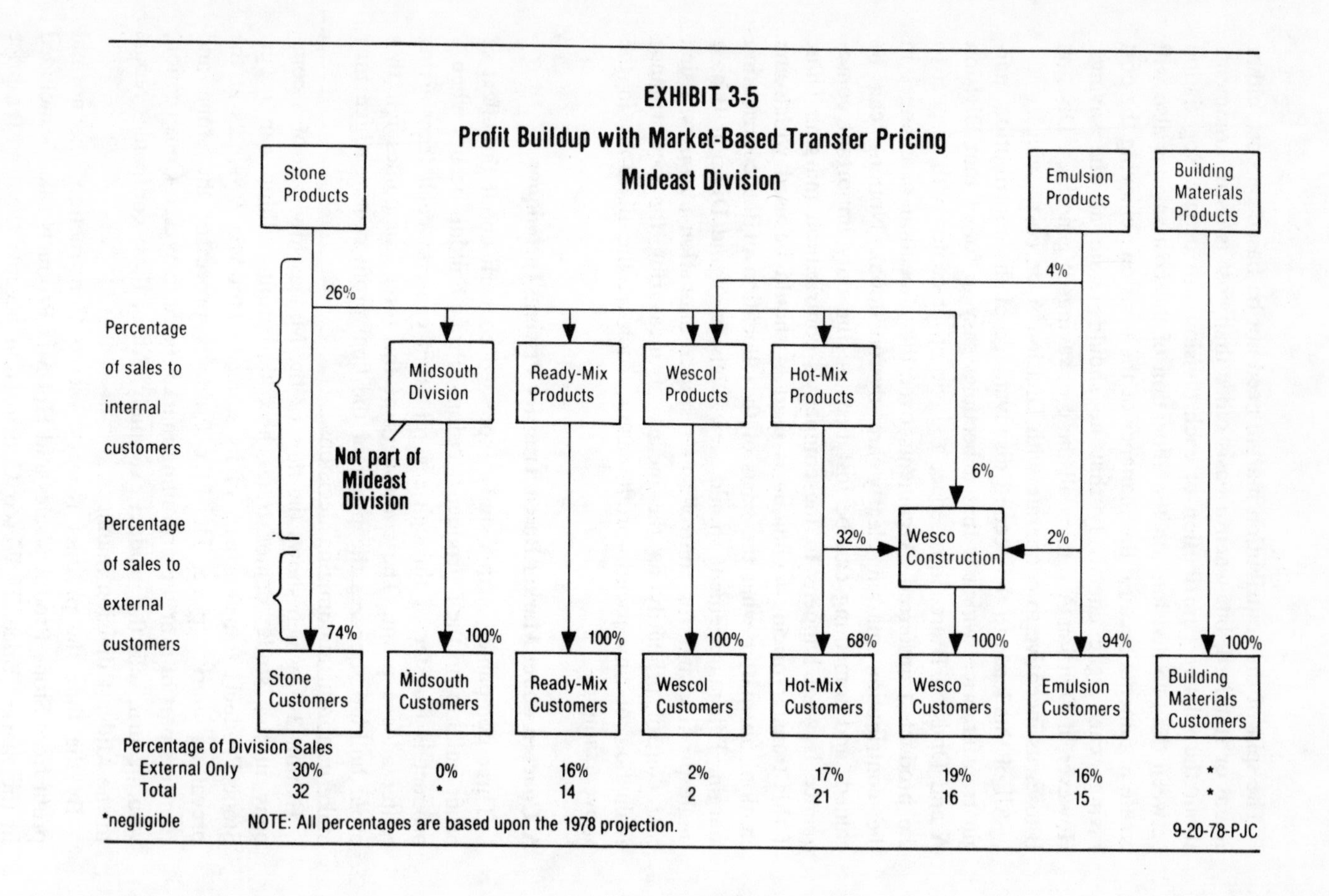

product that would appear to be profitable to the company. For example, assume that Stone Products sells the product externally for $2 per square yard, which includes a $.50 contribution margin, and Hot-Mix Products sells the processed product externally at $6 per square yard, which includes a $2 contribution margin. Finally Wesco Construction sells the product it receives from Hot-Mix Products at $10 per square yard, with a $1 contribution margin. The analysis, together with assumed costs, is shown in Exhibit 3-6.

EXHIBIT 3-6

Profit Buildup in Mideast Division

Stone Products ▶ Hot-Mix Products ▶ Wesco Construction = Company View

	Stone Products	Hot-Mix Products	Wesco Construction		Company View
Sales Price	$2.00	$6	$10		$10.00
Transfer Price		($2)	($6)		
Variable Costs	($1.50)	($2)	($3)		(6.50)
Contribution margin per square yard	$ .50 +	$2 +	$1	=	$3.50

As long as the prevailing market price stays around $10 per square yard, Wesco Construction will buy from Hot-Mix Products, who will buy from Stone Products. Suppose, however, that Wesco Construction faces competitive bidding for a large contract where the expected low bid is below $9 per square yard. Should Wesco Construction bid? From its own view, it should not bid because its contribution margin will become negative. From the company's view, however, it would appear that it should bid as long as the price is greater than $6.50 because the company will have a positive contribution margin. A similar situation might occur if Wesco Construction is allowed to purchase its product externally when Hot-Mix Products cannot supply the product at the prevailing market price because of profit buildup from Stone Products.

The manager of the Mideast division recognized the profit buildup and allowed transfers at below the prevailing market price when competitive situations were involved. In so doing, some of the division managers' successful bids were lower than the bids of another division in the company. The other division strictly followed the company's policy of transferring at the prevailing market price and lost some business to the Mideast division as a result. The company controller referred to the Mideast division's transfer pricing as "creative transfer pricing." In addition, the profit centers were not allowed to adjust transfer prices downward for economies from selling internally. Thus, part of the advantage of vertical integration was ignored, which worked a further hazard on the final profit center's decision process.

It is easy to see in Exhibit 3-6 that transfers from Hot-Mix Products to Wesco Construction should be at the market price. For example, if Wesco Construction cuts its market price to $8 in order to win a bid, the company will earn a contribution margin of $1.50, ($8 – $6.50). If Hot-Mix Products sells its products to its own customers rather than to Wesco Construction, however, the company will earn a contribution margin of $2.50, ($6.00 – $3.50). When the other companies in the Mideast division can sell their products to customers at the market price, they should not sell to Wesco Construction at lower than the market price less economies from selling internally. If they do, the company will not maximize its profit.

Another company in this study, in order to avoid profit buildup that led to lack of competitiveness by the receiving division, allowed negotiation of the transfer price for any product that was transferred across profit center boundaries whenever the receiving profit center was bidding against a competitor whose products did not cross profit center boundaries. The negotiation resulted in a split of the total profit on the product based on the relative contribution of each profit center. This is the negotiated contribution margin transfer pricing technique.

Crossing profit center boundaries does not change things. If the transferred product can be sold at the external market price, that price, less economies from selling internally, should be the transfer price. Determining when the market price is appropriate to use as the transfer price is discussed in Chapter 5.

Summary

This chapter focused on one of the two classes of profit center transfer pricing techniques, market-based techniques. Market-based techniques are based on the prevailing market price; therefore, care should be taken to ensure that the prevailing market is appropriate.

Notes

1. The number of transfer pricing techniques used as the primary transfer pricing technique exceeds the number of companies in the study because several companies were divided into very large segments, each of which developed its own transfer pricing policies. The number of transfer pricing techniques used as secondary techniques is less than the number used as primary transfer pricing techniques because some companies felt their secondary technique involved so little volume it was not important.
2. David Solomons, *Divisional Performance: Measurement and Control,* Financial Executives Research Foundation, New York, 1965, pp. 177-178.
3. Richard J. Schwab, "A Contribution Approach to Transfer Pricing," *Management Accounting,* February 1975, pp. 46-48.

Chapter 4

Nonmarket-Based and Cost Center Transfer Pricing Techniques

This chapter continues the discussion of profit center transfer pricing techniques by focusing on the characteristics, advantages and disadvantages of the second class, nonmarket-based techniques. (See Exhibit 3-1.) Unlike the first class, market-based techniques, nonmarket-based techniques are based on some definition of cost.

Cost center techniques, discussed in the latter half of this chapter, are the second major group of transfer pricing techniques. Although cost center techniques are related to nonmarket-based techniques in that both use some definition of cost, unlike nonmarket-based techniques, cost center techniques do not allow a responsibility center a profit. Both cost center and nonmarket-based techniques have certain advantages although none of these techniques is satisfactory in all situations.

Profit Center Transfer Pricing Techniques: Nonmarket-Based

Nonmarket-based transfer pricing techniques are based on some definition of cost. The word "cost" should not be taken too literally here. Of the three nonmarket-based techniques—opportunity cost, marginal cost, and cost-plus — only the latter uses cost in an accounting or conventional sense. The other two techniques use a special definition of cost.

Only three of the companies in this study used a nonmarket-based transfer pricing technique as their primary technique, while five companies used a nonmarket-based technique as their secondary technique. The cost-plus transfer pricing technique used by seven companies is the only nonmarket-based technique that has received any wide use.

The other two nonmarket-based techniques, opportunity cost and marginal cost, are discussed for special reasons. Opportunity cost is discussed because it forms the foundation for the recommendations in Chapter 5 and marginal cost because it has been widely suggested as a useful transfer pricing technique.

Opportunity Cost

Opportunity cost is defined as a measure of the sacrifice made (in the form of opportunities foregone) in order to pursue a particular course of action. Thus, in an accounting sense, opportunity cost is not really a cost. The cost of one course of action is measured in terms of what was given up by not following the next best course of action. Some examples of opportunity cost are shown below.

> If an asset can be used to perform only one function and it cannot be used in other ways or sold as scrap, the opportunity costs of that asset are zero. Thus, the opportunity costs of using the underground gas pipe of a gas company in the city of Chicago are zero because the pipe is going to carry gas and nothing but gas in Chicago. As long as the revenues from carrying the gas are greater than the incremental costs connected with delivering the gas, it will be desirable for the company to continue to deliver the gas. The costs of using the pipe are zero because there are no alternative opportunities. In a theoretical as well as physical sense, the costs of the gas pipe are sunk; the pipe has zero opportunity cost.
>
> A machine used to make product A will have an opportunity cost if the machine can be sold or if it can also make product B. For example, assume that a period's production of B can be sold for $10,000 and that the costs which vary directly with production are $8,000. The period's opportunity cost of not producing product B is $2,000. The proceeds that are forsaken by producing A instead of B are actually a cost of producing A. The opportunity cost principle is extremely useful in deciding on alternative uses of productive facilities.[1]

The last sentence above states precisely why an opportunity cost transfer pricing technique can be useful: an opportunity cost technique, properly utilized, will help select from alternative uses of productive facilities while simultaneously guiding decision makers toward profit maximization for the firm. A simple example can illustrate this idea.

Assume that Division A manufactures two products, X and Y. Product X sells in the market for $10 and has variable costs of $6. Product Y cannot be sold in the open market but must be transferred to Division B. Division A incurs $4 of variable cost on Product Y before it is transferred to Division B. Division B further processes the product, adding $2 more in variable cost, and sells the final product for $12. This situation is summarized in Exhibit 4-1 (page 52).

The total contribution margin on Product X is $400, and Division A receives all of it because it both manufactures and sells the product. The total contribution of Product Y is $600, but it is split between Divisions A and B. Division A has a negative contribution margin of $400 on Product Y, while Division B has a positive contribution margin of $1,000 on Product Y.

As a profit center, Division A would prefer to produce only Product X because it receives a positive contribution margin of $400 for 100 units of the product. Division A could increase its total contribution to $800 by producing 100 more units of Product X instead of producing Product Y. Product Y is more profitable to the company than Product X, however, since the CM/PU on Product Y is $6. One way to solve this dilemma is to set the transfer price equal to the sum of the variable cost incurred by Division A on Product Y and the opportunity cost of Product X. The opportunity cost of Product X is the contribution margin per unit of $4 that Division A does not receive when it produces Product Y with manufacturing facilities that could be used to produce Product X. The analysis is shown in Exhibit 4-2 (page 53).

The transfer price is set at $8, the sum of the variable cost per unit of Product Y ($4 VC-A) and the opportunity cost of not producing Product X ($4 CM/PU). Now Division A receives a $4 per unit contribution margin for producing Product Y and selling it internally. Division B receives a contribution margin of $2 per unit when Product Y is sold externally.

The company will want to continue producing Product Y as long as the contribution margin of $600 is greater than any other opportunity. For example, suppose Division B could use its productive capacity to manufacture 100 units of Product Z with a contribution margin of $3 per unit. Division B should produce Product Z and discontinue buying Product Y from Division A. Division A should discontinue making Product Y since it cannot be sold externally and produce only Product X. This procedure will maximize the company's profits. Before Product Z was produced, the company's profit was $1,000 [$400 (Product X) + $600 (Product Y)]. With Product Z the profit will be $1,100 [($4 CM/PU) (200 units Product X) + ($3 CM/PU) (100 units Product Z)].

The unique feature of opportunity cost is that when it is included in the cost of the products being produced, profit maximization is easier. For example, the company's increase in total profit due to Product Y

EXHIBIT 4-1

Summary of Sales for Products X and Y

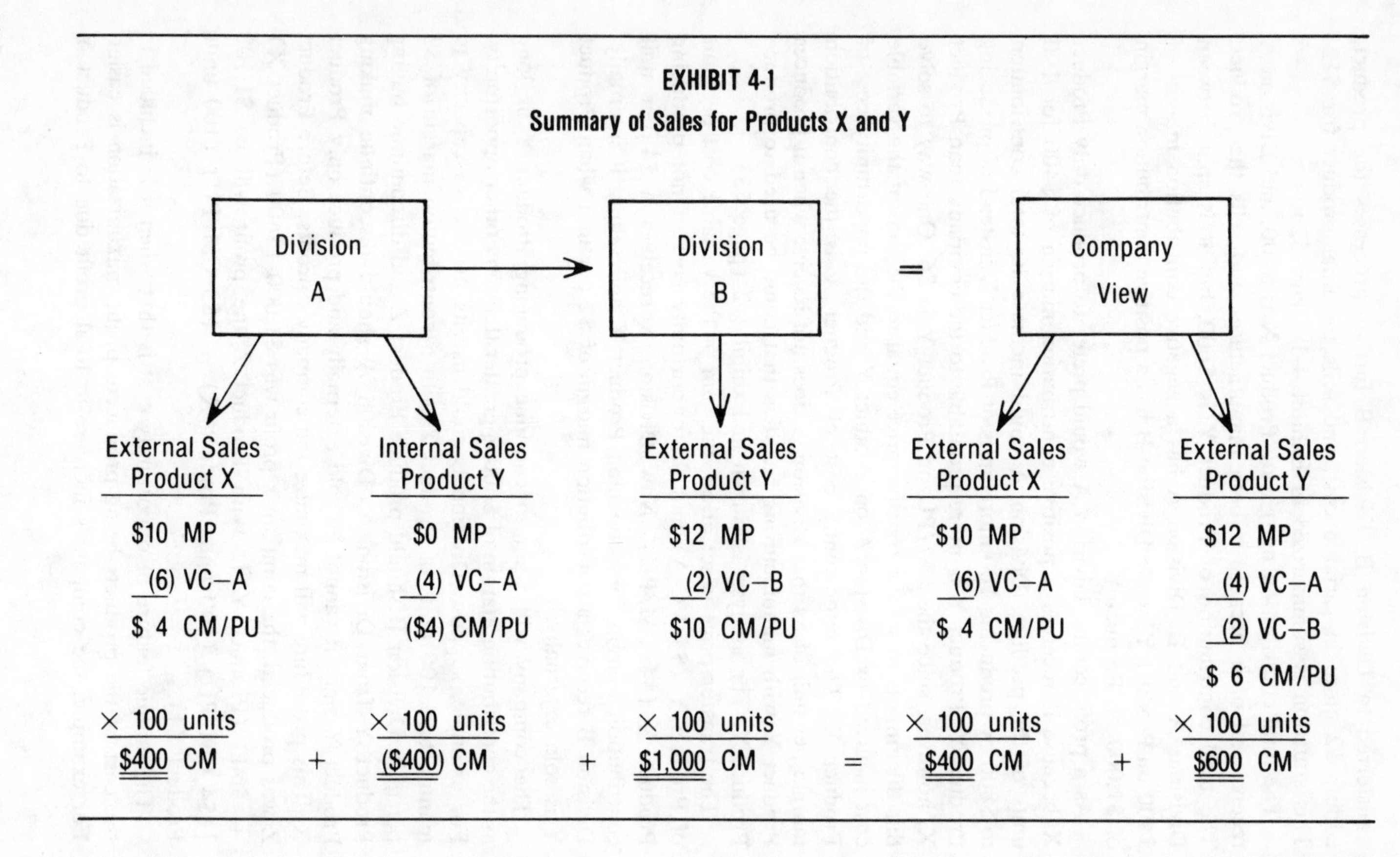

EXHIBIT 4-2
Opportunity Cost Transfer Pricing

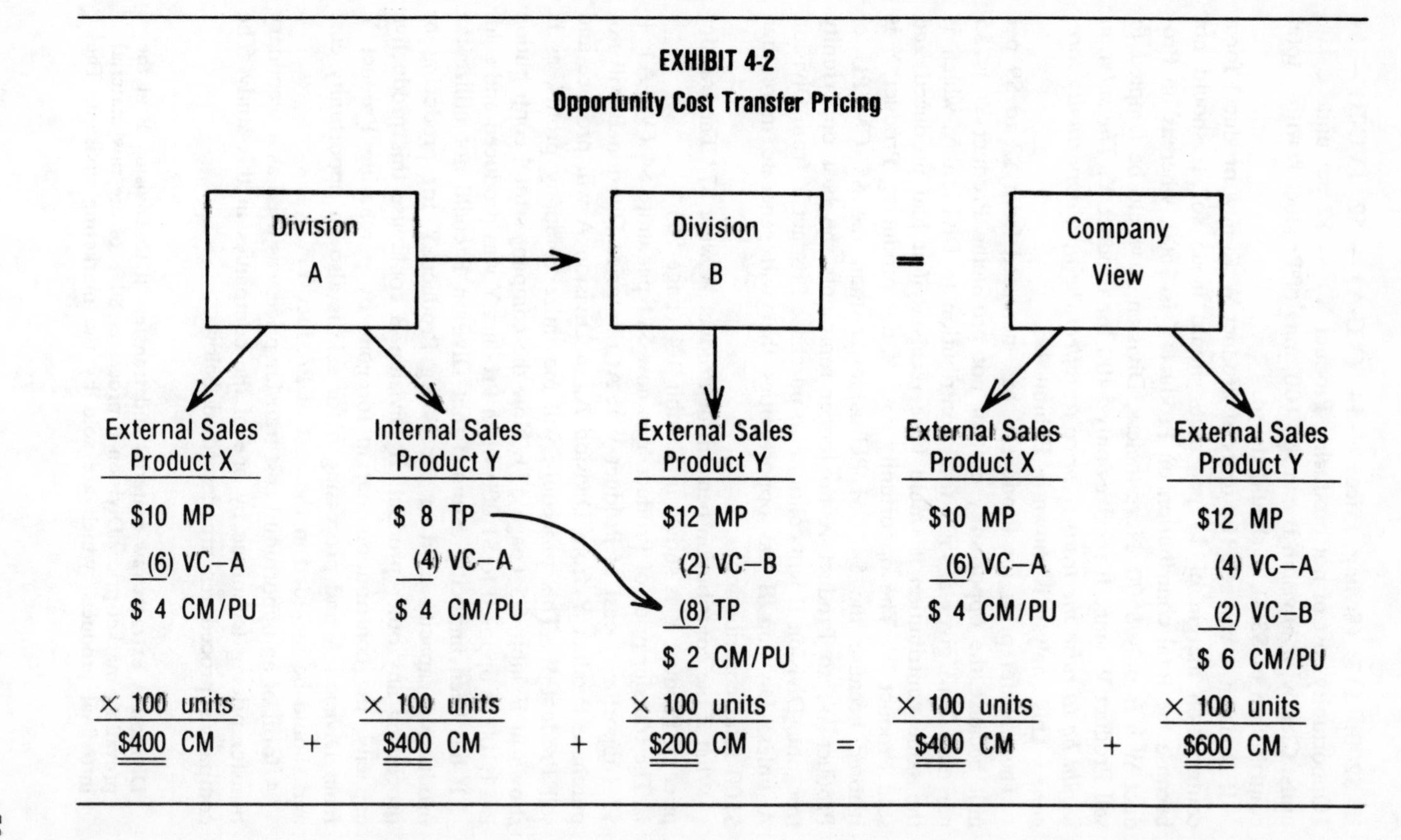

is \$200: \$12 (Selling Price) — \$4 (VC-A) — \$2 (VC-B) — \$4 (Opportunity cost of not producing Product X) = \$2 per unit × 100 units. Clearly, if Division B can sell 100 units of Product Z with a total contribution of \$300, it should do so.

If Division A can sell 100 units of Product W (a new product) for a contribution margin of \$5 per unit, should it do so? It should not because the total contribution on Product Y is \$600, whereas on Product W it is only \$500. Nevertheless, Division A would be tempted to sell Product W since it receives only \$400 for Product Y. *The solution would be to raise the transfer price to reflect the new opportunity foregone.*[2] This analysis is shown in Exhibit 4-3.

The transfer price for Product Y has increased from \$8 to \$9 per unit because the opportunity cost of not producing Product W is \$5 per unit. This gives a \$500 total contribution to Division A, which is the same contribution it would have received if it had produced and sold Product W. The opportunity cost of not producing Product X is ignored because the \$4 CM/PU is lower than the \$5 CM/PU of Product W, so Product X no longer represents the best opportunity foregone. Division B will continue to purchase Product Y from Division A unless Division B has opportunities that will generate more than \$100 total contribution.

What if the contribution per unit of Product W were \$7? The transfer price of Product Y is shown in Exhibit 4-4 (page 56).

The transfer price of Product Y is now \$11 per unit: \$4 (VC-A) + \$7 (opportunity cost of Product W). At this price Division B will not purchase Product Y from Division A, so Division A will produce and sell Product W. This procedure will maximize company profits, as is shown in Exhibit 4-5 (page 57). Now the company's total contribution is \$1,100 as opposed to \$1,000 when Product Y was produced and sold.

It has been implicitly assumed that Division B could not utilize the productive capacity used in processing Product Y for producing or processing any other product. If Division B could use this productive capacity, the contribution margin foregone by purchasing Product Y from Division A and processing it for sale is also an opportunity cost and should be included in the cost of Product Y.[3]

A form of an opportunity cost transfer price was used as a secondary transfer pricing technique by one of the companies in this study. The company's procedures are described below:

> Division A extracts raw material and transfers it to Division B at the prevailing market price. Division B processes 80% of the raw material into final products, which are sold by the marketing division. The

EXHIBIT 4-3

Product W Opportunity Cost Transfer Pricing

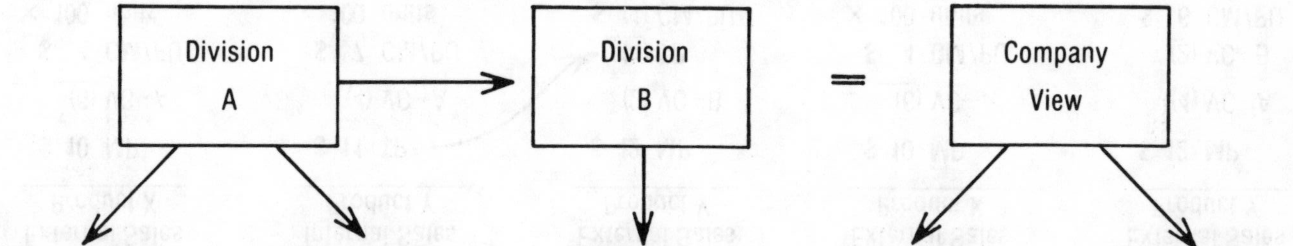

Division A → Division B = Company View

Division A: External Sales Product X		Division A: Internal Sales Product Y		Division B: External Sales Product Y		Company View: External Sales Product X		Company View: External Sales Product Y
$ 10 MP		$ 9 TP		$ 12 MP		$ 10 MP		$ 12 MP
(6) VC—A		(4) VC—A		(2) VC—B		(6) VC—A		(4) VC—A
$ 4 CM/PU		$ 5 CM/PU		(9) TP		$ 4 CM/PU		(2) VC—B
× 100 units		× 100 units		$ 1 CM/PU		× 100 units		$ 6 CM/PU
				× 100 units				× 100 units
$400 CM	+	$500 CM	+	$100 CM	=	$400 CM	+	$600 CM

EXHIBIT 4-4
Product W with a Contribution Per Unit of $7

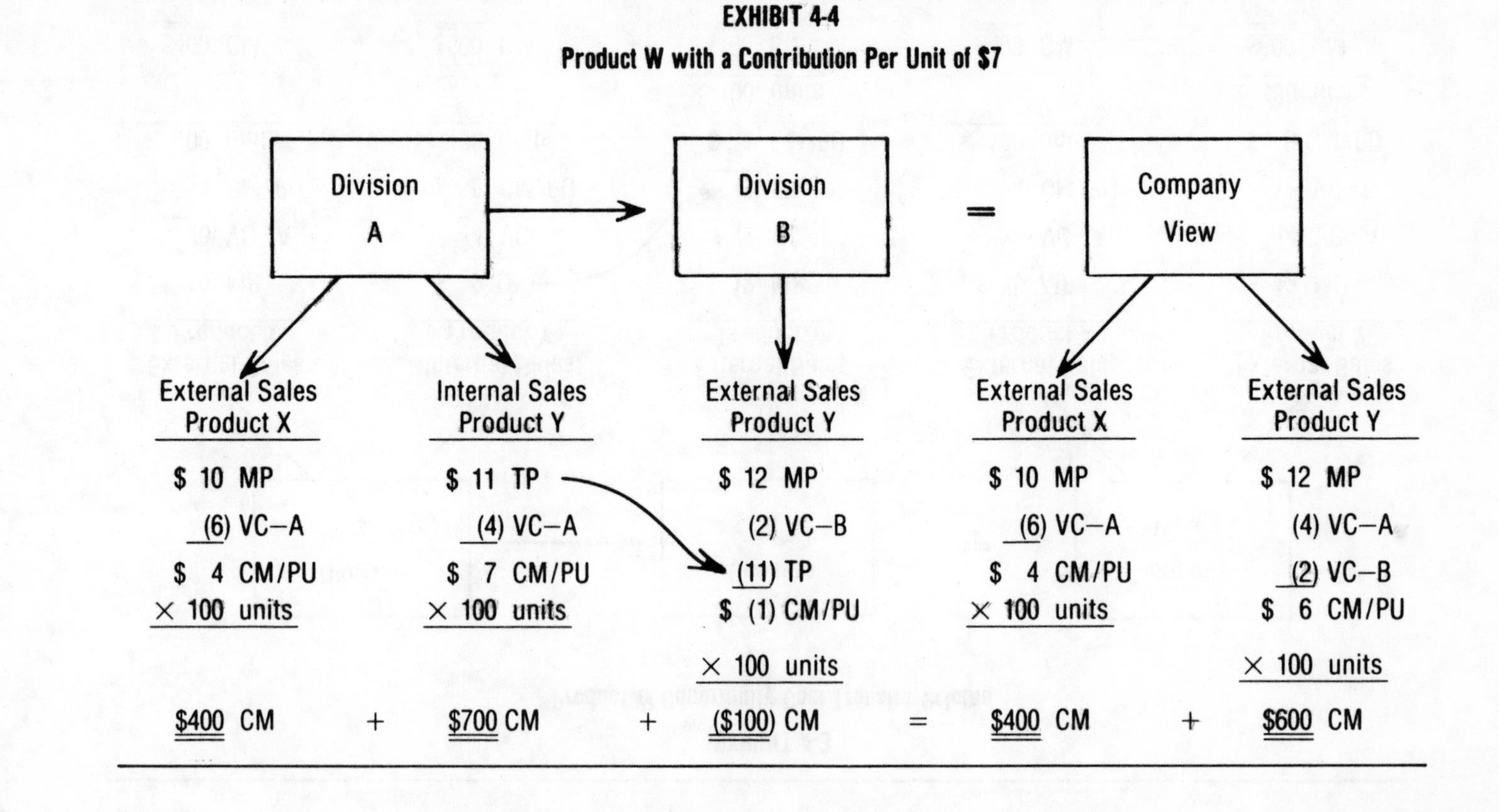

EXHIBIT 4-5
Maximizing Company Profits with Product W

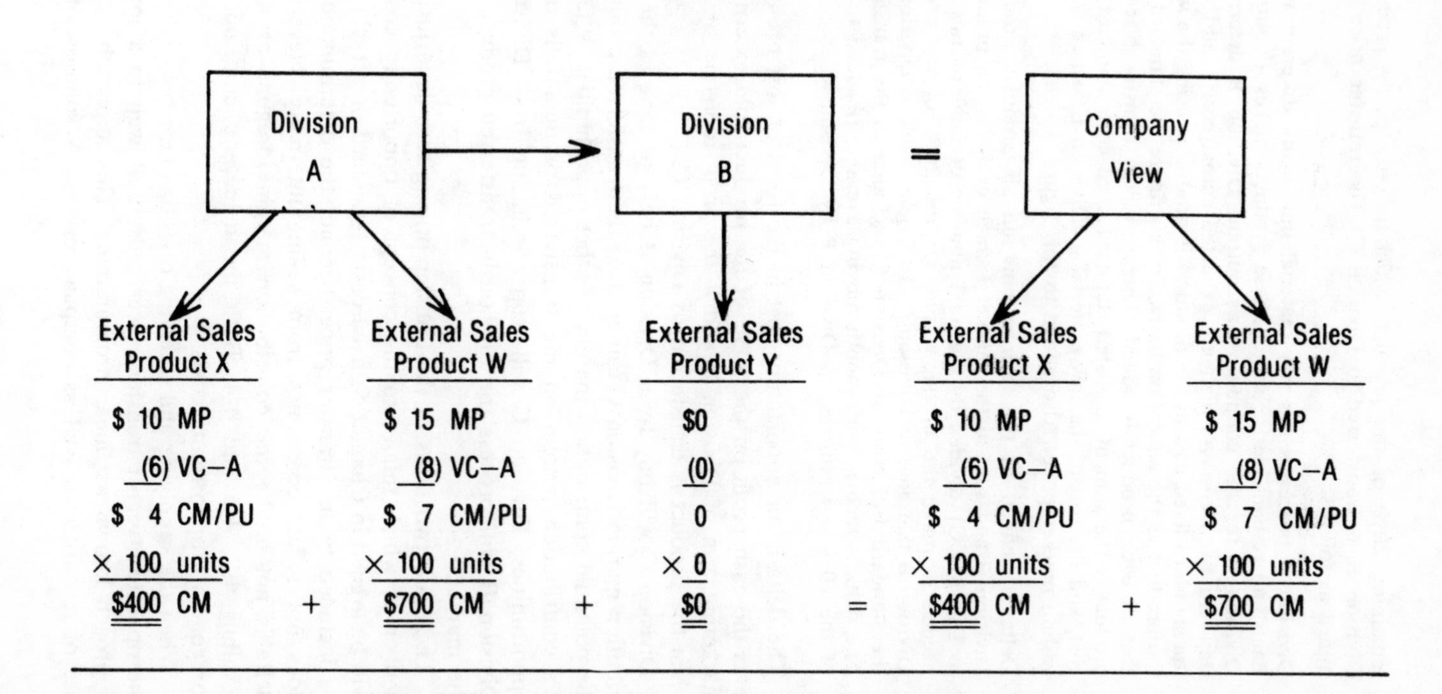

remaining 20% of the product, which is only partly processed by Division B, is transferred to Division C. The transfer price is determined as follows:

> Division B processes the raw material into many different products. Each unit responsible for selling these products makes a contract with Division B for the coming year's output. Division B determines its standard fixed costs (which are expected actual costs) and allocates the standard fixed cost to the products it produces, using the weight of the product as the allocation basis. To this figure the standard variable cost of each product is added. Therefore, the transfer price of any product is the sum of allocated standard fixed cost, standard variable cost, and the cost of the raw material to Division B, which is the prevailing market price. Also added to this figure is delta.
>
> Delta is defined as the cash income on all products produced by Division B and sold in the market (which excludes the products sold to Division C) divided by the total number of units of raw material needed to make the products sold. Of the 20% of the product of Division B that goes to Division C, 10% goes back to Division B with the standard full costs of Division C included in the transfer price. The delta, which is a 12-month moving average, is added to the cost of the 10% not returned to Division B by Division C.

The delta is an opportunity cost in the form of lost profit. It represents the cash profit on the 90% of the product sold externally by the marketing arm of Division B and is the profit foregone by Division B when the product is transferred to Division C.

Division C will buy from Division B only as long as the total contribution margin Division C can earn on the transferred product exceeds the potential contribution margin of other opportunities. When Division C's contribution margin on the transferred product falls below other opportunities, Division C will stop purchasing from Division B, and Division B will process the previously transferred product for sale in the market.

There are two flaws in the transfer pricing technique just described, neither of which relates to the concept of opportunity cost. First, as will be argued in Chapter 5, fixed costs (standard or actual) should not be included in the transfer price. Second, the determination of profit does not reflect economies from selling internally. Nevertheless, the delta is not unlike the contribution margin foregone as described in Exhibits 4-2, 4-3 and 4-4. Both the delta and contribution margin foregone are opportunity costs.

When the supplying and receiving divisions face resource constraints, the opportunity cost transfer price lends itself well to a mathematical approach known as linear programming. This approach optimizes the use of resources as well as company profits. A solution of allocating the contribution margin is arrived at mathematically, and considers the productive constraints of the divisions involved. This approach, however, while very useful, is too complex for discussion here except in an elementary way, which would not be particularly enlightening. The reader is referred to Mohamed Onsi[4] for further information.

The principal advantage of the opportunity cost transfer price is that it motivates the operating managers involved toward maximizing company profits. This is a strong advantage. Unfortunately, however, the opportunity cost transfer pricing technique has a number of disadvantages that have limited its usefulness.

First, the concept of opportunity cost is somewhat difficult to grasp. How can an opportunity not taken be a cost of an opportunity that is taken? Furthermore, opportunity costs are by their very nature rather "iffy." Simply determining the alternative courses of action can be difficult and subjective.

Second, the additional profit (or cost saved) that would be earned by an alternative course is hard to determine. Opportunity costs often are not measured in accounting records either because some of the costs are not considered costs by accountants or because the transactions involved are not recorded on the company's records. Hence, the data often are difficult to obtain.

Third, the opportunity cost is always zero when there is no alternative course of action, but a transfer price of zero clearly is inadequate. Opportunity costs need to be combined with other costs, such as incremental costs or variable costs, to form transfer prices.

If these disadvantages can be overcome, the opportunity cost transfer pricing technique holds a lot of promise. Indeed, the opportunity cost technique forms the foundation for the recommendations in Chapter 5.

Marginal Cost

Although none of the companies in this study used a marginal cost transfer price, it is still an important concept because it has long been accepted as the theoretically correct transfer price in several situations.[5] The concepts of marginal cost and marginal revenue are discussed briefly, followed by a discussion of why the marginal cost is not used more frequently as a transfer price.

Marginal cost is defined as the change in total cost that results from a small change in output.[6] Total cost is the sum of total fixed cost and total variable cost. Because fixed costs do not change with changes in output, the change in total cost is due entirely to a change in variable cost. Marginal cost is computed by dividing the change in total cost (or change in total variable cost) by the unit change in output that gives rise to the cost change. This procedure determines the additional cost per unit of the resulting increase in output. An example of determining marginal cost for the Ace Manufacturing Co. is shown in Exhibit 4-6.

EXHIBIT 4-6
Determining Marginal Cost
Ace Manufacturing Co.

A No. of Units (Given)	B Total Fixed Cost (Given)	C Total Var- Costs (Given)	D Total Cost (B+C)	E Change In Total Cost ΔD	F Marginal Cost ΔD÷ΔA
0	$300	$ 0	$ 300	$ 0	$ 0
1	300	150	450	150	150
2	300	250	550	100	100
3	300	325	625	75	75
4	300	375	675	50	50
5	300	425	725	50	50
6	300	500	800	75	75
7	300	650	950	150	150
8	300	850	1,150	200	200
9	300	1,150	1,450	300	300

ΔA = the change in column A

ΔD = the change in column D

Notice that for the Ace Manufacturing Co. the marginal cost falls from $150 per unit to $50 per unit as the number of units produced increases from 0 to 4. This change is caused by Ace's efficient combination of productive factors, capital and labor, such that the amount of the productive factors necessary to produce unit two is less than was necessary to produce unit one, the amount of productive factors necessary to produce unit three is less than was necessary to produce unit two, and so forth.

Starting with unit six, Ace's marginal cost begins to increase, thus giving the marginal cost curve a U-shaped look (see Exhibit 4-8). In actual production situations, it is this second part of the marginal cost curve, the increasing part, that the Ace Manufacturing Co. will see. A business that is able to produce an additional unit at less than the preceding unit will do so and will keep doing so until the marginal cost begins increasing (assuming, of course, that the units can be sold). The question then becomes when is it uneconomical for Ace to produce more units. The answer is that it is uneconomical when the additional cost of a unit produced by Ace (marginal cost) exceeds the additional revenue Ace receives from the sale of the unit (marginal revenue). In other words, Ace should produce until marginal cost equals marginal revenue (MC = MR).

Marginal revenue, which is defined as the change in total revenue brought about by a small change in output, should not be confused with the sales price. If a firm sells 10 units at $9 per unit for total revenue of $90 and then lowers the price per unit to $8 in order to sell 20 units, the increase in revenue is $70, ($160 – $90). Marginal revenue is this increase divided by the increase in sales (10 units), or $7 per unit. The relationship between Ace's marginal cost and marginal revenue is shown in Exhibit 4-7 (page 62).

According to Exhibit 4-7, the Ace Manufacturing Co. should produce the sixth unit, but not the seventh. If it produces the seventh unit, the marginal cost of producing the unit ($150) will exceed the marginal revenue from the sale of the unit ($75), resulting in a loss of $75.

Notice that Ace's total contribution margin increases from $0 to a high of $475 with a total of six units produced. If it produces more than six units, the total contribution margin will decline until finally it becomes negative.

In Exhibit 4-7, Ace's marginal revenue declined steadily from $225 for the first unit to $25 for the ninth unit. This decline is an example of imperfect competition because the more units Ace produces, the lower the price it must charge in order to induce customers to purchase the units. Graphically this is shown in Exhibit 4-8 (page 63).

But suppose that Ace does not have to lower its sales price per unit in order to induce customers to purchase additional units. In this case Ace would face perfect competition. Let's assume that Ace can sell all the units it produces at a price of $175. This situation is shown in Exhibit 4-9 (page 63).

According to Exhibit 4-9, Ace should produce seven units rather than six because the marginal cost of the seventh unit ($150) does not exceed the marginal revenue ($175). However, Ace should not produce the eighth unit.

EXHIBIT 4-7
Marginal Cost and Marginal Revenue
Ace Manufacturing Co.

A No. of Units (Given)	B Selling Price Per Unit (Given)	C Total Revenue (A×B)	D Marginal Revenue (ΔC)	E Marginal Cost (Exhibit 4-6)	F Marginal Profit (D−E)	G Company Contribution Margin ΣF
0			0	0	0	0
1	225	225	225	150	75	75
2	212.50	425	200	100	100	175
3	200	600	175	75	100	275
4	187.50	750	150	50	100	375
5	175	875	125	50	75	450
6	162.50	975	100	75	25	475
7	150	1,050	75	150	(75)	400
8	137.50	1,100	50	200	(150)	250
9	125	1,125	25	300	(275)	(25)

ΔC = the change in column C
ΣF = the sum of column F

The usefulness of marginal cost in transfer pricing stems from the relationship of marginal cost and marginal revenue. If it is not economical to produce when marginal cost exceeds marginal revenue, then the point where marginal cost equals marginal revenue maximizes company profit. A transfer price determined by this point will achieve profit maximization.

Unfortunately, the concept of marginal cost often is difficult to apply to daily business problems. One of the most important problems is that marginal costs are difficult to obtain. In order to calculate a marginal cost schedule, the costs of a wide range of production activity are necessary, but companies rarely produce over a very wide range of productive activity. Instead, they tend to produce around some fairly stable level of production, with the result being that costs associated with very low or very high levels of production are merely educated guesses.

An equally important problem is that marginal costs do not always occur in actual business situations the same way that textbooks depict

EXHIBIT 4-8
Imperfect Competition

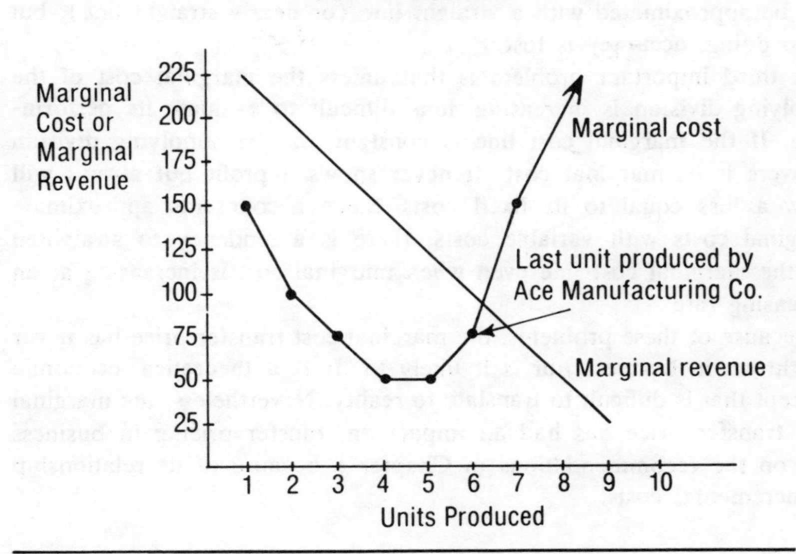

EXHIBIT 4-9
Perfect Competition

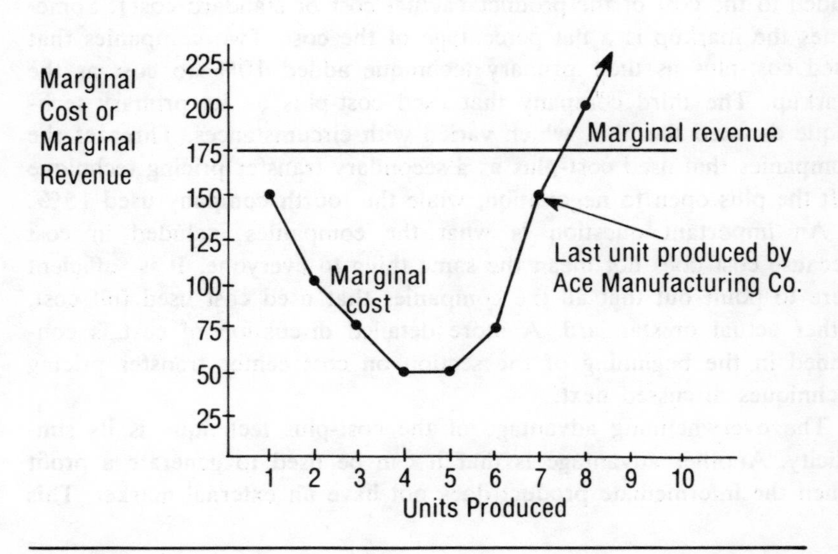

them as occurring. Fixed costs are not stable over wide ranges of production. As profitability increases, discretionary fixed costs are added.[7] Costs that are semivariable sometimes occur in a stepladder form that can be approximated with a straight line (or nearly straight line), but in so doing, accuracy is lost.

A third important problem is that unless the marginal cost of the supplying division is increasing, it is difficult to evaluate its performance. If the marginal cost line is constant, all the supplying division recovers is its marginal cost. It never shows a profit but always will show a loss equal to its fixed costs. Since accountants approximate marginal costs with variable costs, there is a tendency to straighten out the marginal cost line even when marginal cost is increasing at an increasing rate.

Because of these problems, the marginal cost transfer price has never caught on in business nor is it likely to. It is a theoretical economic concept that is difficult to translate to reality. Nevertheless, the marginal cost transfer price has had an impact on transfer pricing in business and on the recommendations in Chapter 5 because of its relationship to incremental costs.

Cost-Plus

Three companies in this study used the cost-plus transfer price as the primary transfer pricing technique, and four others used it as a secondary technique. It is a simple transfer pricing technique. A markup is added to the cost of the product (actual cost or standard cost). Sometimes the markup is a flat percentage of the cost. Two companies that used cost-plus as their primary technique added 10% to cost as the markup. The third company that used cost-plus as its primary technique dictated the plus, which varied with circumstances. Three of the companies that used cost-plus as a secondary transfer pricing technique left the plus open to negotiation, while the fourth company used 15%.

An important question is what the companies included in cost because cost does not mean the same thing to everyone. It is sufficient here to point out that all the companies that used cost used full cost, either actual or standard. A more detailed discussion of cost is contained in the beginning of the section on cost center transfer pricing techniques discussed next.

The overwhelming advantage of the cost-plus technique is its simplicity. Another advantage is that it can be used to generate a profit when the intermediate product does not have an external market. This use is particularly advantageous with profit centers because managers in profit centers will be unenthusiastic about producing products for another division when cost is all that is recovered. Cost-plus results in pseudo-profit centers, however, and if pseudo-profit centers are acceptable, the allocation of the company's contribution margin on the product is probably a better technique.

A third advantage is that the accounting involved in cost-plus is quite simple. Transfers can be made at cost and the markup added periodically when necessary. Formal journal entries of the markup may not even be necessary.

The main disadvantage of the cost-plus transfer pricing technique is the arbitrary nature of the markup. This disadvantage is indeed significant. Unless the markups are tied into some economic reality, such as the prevailing market price, suboptimization of company profits will occur. If the markups can be tied to economic reality, however, there is little reason to use a cost-plus technique. For example, if the markup is designed to approximate the adjusted market price, the company would be better off to use the adjusted market price as the transfer price.

Another disadvantage of the cost-plus technique is that using a flat percentage of cost to determine the dollar value of the markup will lead directly to higher costs unless cost control is exercised by another means such as standard costing. Otherwise, the higher the cost, the higher the markup. In total, the cost-plus technique, in spite of its fairly wide use, has little to recommend it.

Cost Center Transfer Pricing Techniques

There are fewer cost center transfer pricing techniques than profit center techniques because there are a limited number of views as to what constitutes the cost of an intermediate product. Cost can be classified into two broad categories, actual cost and standard cost, with each subdivided into variable cost and full cost.

What constitutes the transferred-out cost of a product varies from company to company. Most of the companies used standard cost, with the standard established to approximate actual costs. In no instance did the standard costs originate from studies of what the cost of producing the product should be. Rather, actual costs were estimated for the coming year and treated as standard costs. In fact, they were budgeted standards that changed every year.

None of the companies used just variable costs, either actual or standard, as the transfer price. All companies, including those using an allocation of the contribution margin based on standard full cost and cost-plus, allocated actual or standard fixed costs to the product. Hence, one division's fixed costs became another division's variable costs. This process obscures profit analysis, as the following illustration will show.

Assume that a company produces and sells two products, X and Y. The products are produced in Division A and transferred to Division B at full cost. (Division B is strictly a marketing division.) The cost figures are as follows:

Products	Units	Sales Price	*Variable Costs* Division A	Division B	Fixed Costs
X	100	$11	$3	$3	$1,000
X	100	$16	$7	$3	

In Part A of Exhibit 4-10, it is assumed that Division A allocates fixed costs to Products X and Y according to the variable costs of each and transfers the products to Division B. The analysis shows that from the viewpoint of Division B, Product Y should not be purchased since it leaves Division B with a loss of $100 on the product. From the company view, however, Product Y should be produced and sold since its contribution margin is $600.

In Part B of Exhibit 4-10 (page 68), it is assumed that Division A allocates fixed costs according to the weight of each product. One unit of Product X weighs 1.5 pounds; one unit of Product Y weighs 1 pound. Division B believes now that Product X is the least profitable of the two although the profitability of the company is still $100. Which of the two products is more profitable? Product Y is still more profitable because it has a contribution margin of $600 versus $500 for Product X.

The illustration was fairly simple. In actual business situations the process is more involved. Nevertheless, the result is the same in both simple and complex situations: profitability analysis is obscured. Thus, if fixed costs are included in the transfer price, the receiving division will treat them as variable costs and thereby obscure its profitability analysis. This process eventually will lead to suboptimization of profits.

What should be done with the fixed costs? They should be treated as *period* costs and not *product* costs and transferred to Division B separately. This idea is shown in Exhibit 4-11 (page 69).

Now profitability analysis is not obscured. Division B can use the contribution margin as a means of assessing the profitability of Prod-

EXHIBIT 4-10
Allocating Fixed Costs

Part A—Allocation by Variable Costs

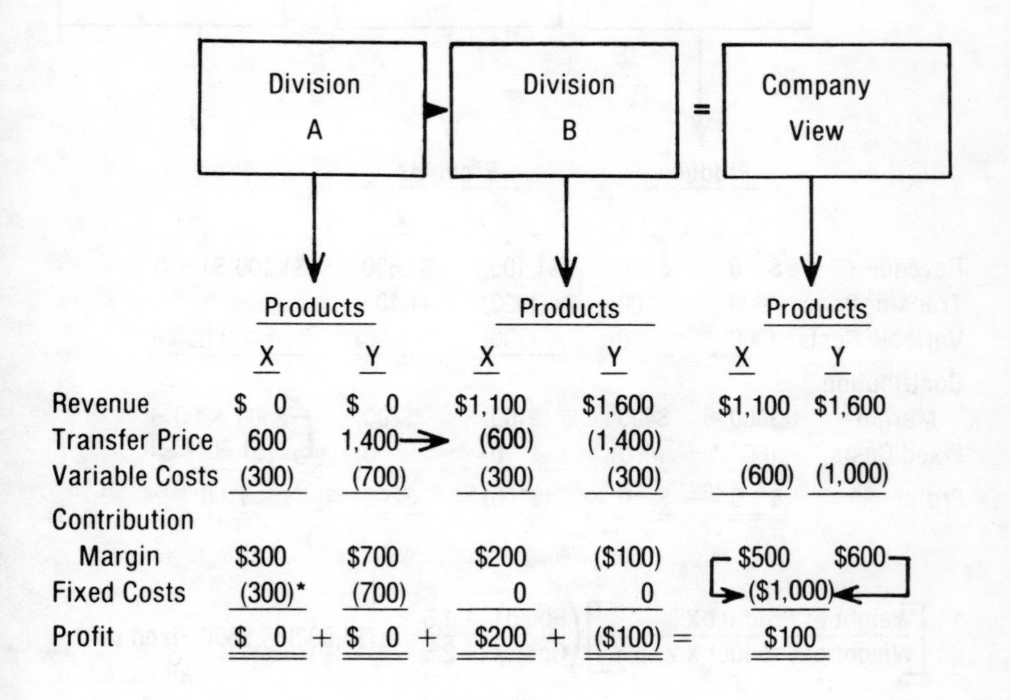

	Division A Products X	Division A Products Y	Division B Products X	Division B Products Y	Company View Products X	Company View Products Y
Revenue	$ 0	$ 0	$1,100	$1,600	$1,100	$1,600
Transfer Price	600	1,400 →	(600)	(1,400)		
Variable Costs	(300)	(700)	(300)	(300)	(600)	(1,000)
Contribution Margin	$300	$700	$200	($100)	$500	$600
Fixed Costs	(300)*	(700)	0	0	($1,000)	
Profit	$ 0 +	$ 0 +	$200 +	($100) =	$100	

* $\left[\frac{\text{Variable Cost Product X}}{\text{Variable Cost X and Y}}\right]\left(\begin{matrix}\text{Fixed}\\\text{Costs}\end{matrix}\right)$ $\frac{\$300}{\$1,000}$ (\$1,000) = \$300 Fixed cost allocated to Product X

\$1,000–\$300 = \$700 Fixed cost allocated to Product Y

Part B—Allocation by Weight

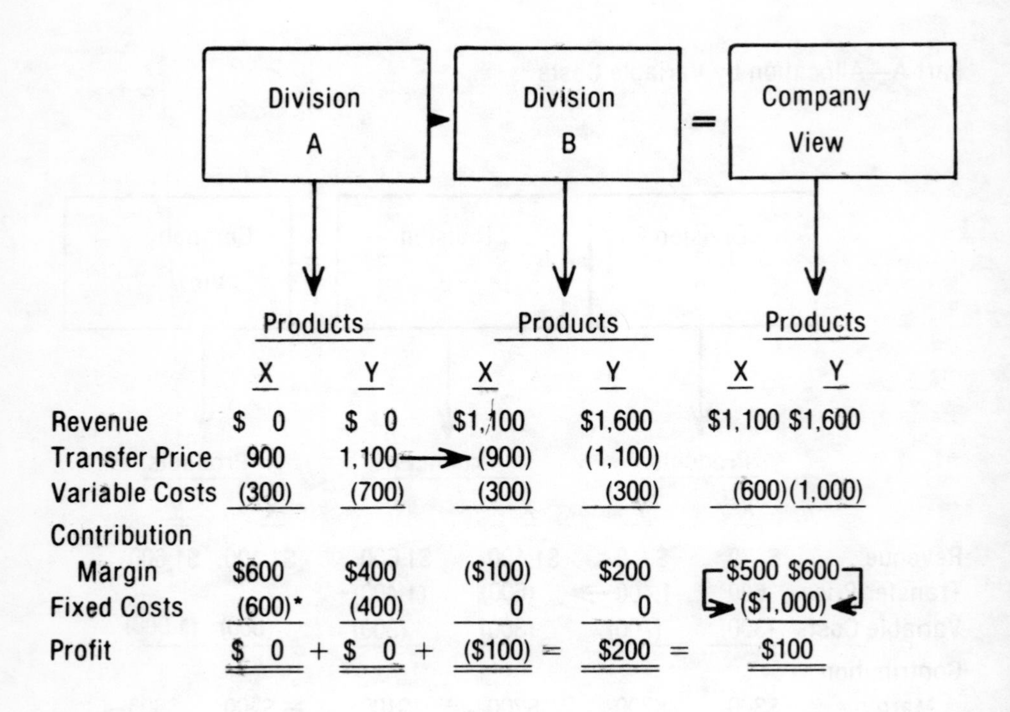

	Division A Products		Division B Products		Company View Products	
	X	Y	X	Y	X	Y
Revenue	$ 0	$ 0	$1,100	$1,600	$1,100	$1,600
Transfer Price	900	1,100 →	(900)	(1,100)		
Variable Costs	(300)	(700)	(300)	(300)	(600)	(1,000)
Contribution Margin	$600	$400	($100)	$200	$500	$600
Fixed Costs	(600)*	(400)	0	0	($1,000)	
Profit	$ 0 +	$ 0 +	($100) =	$200 =	$100	

* $\left[\frac{\text{Weight of Product X}}{\text{Weight of Product X and Y}}\right]\left(\frac{\text{Fixed}}{\text{Costs}}\right)$ $\frac{1.5}{2.5}$ ($1,000) = $600 Fixed cost allocated to Product X

$1,000–$600 = $400 Fixed cost allocated to Product Y

EXHIBIT 4-11
Fixed Costs as Period Costs

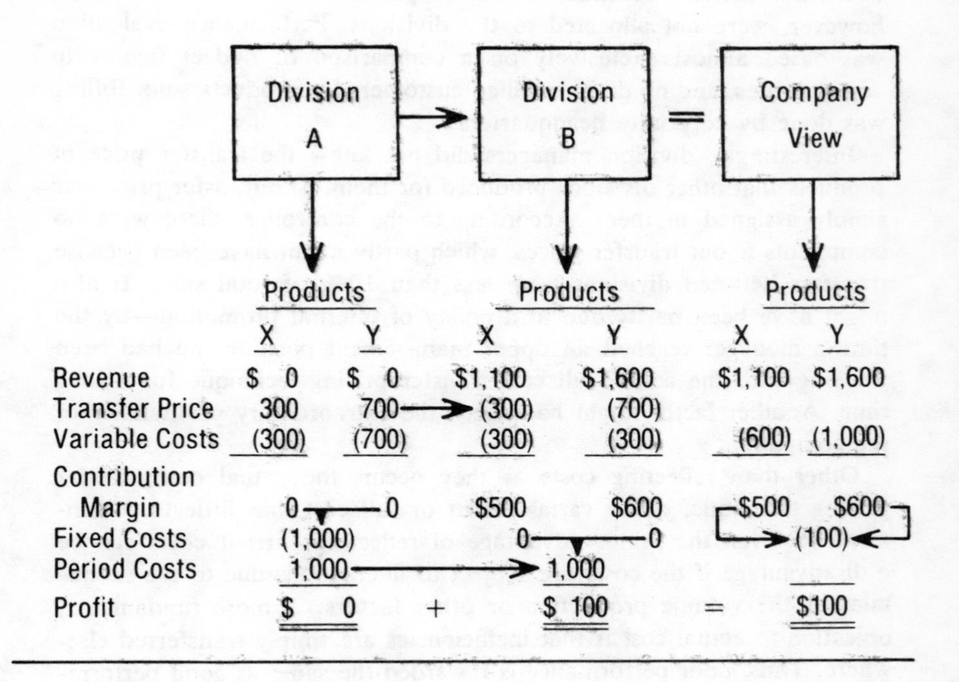

ucts X and Y. The disadvantage of including fixed costs in the transfer price on a per unit basis should be kept in mind as the two cost center transfer pricing techniques are discussed.

Actual Full Cost

One large company used actual full cost as the primary transfer pricing technique in every area. The company was, in the words of the controller, "highly decentralized down to the division level," which was the first level below corporate headquarters. There was less decentralization within the 40 major divisions.

All divisions were profit centers, so all sales revenue for the products assigned to a division accrued to the division. If a product assigned to one division was made by another division, actual direct costs, including direct divisional overhead and a share of indirect divisional overhead, were assigned to the product. Divisional overhead consisted of overhead incurred by the division, corporate overhead that could be traced to divisional activities, and an allocated share of the remaining corporate overhead. Interest revenue, interest expense, and bad debt expense, however, were not allocated to the divisions. Performance evaluation was based almost exclusively on a comparison of budget figures to actual figures, and no division billed customers for products sold. Billing was done by corporate headquarters.

Interestingly, division managers did not know the transfer price of products that other divisions produced for them. The transfer price was simply assigned to them. According to the controller, there were no complaints about transfer prices, which partly might have been because transfers between divisions were less than 10% of total sales. It also might have been partly due to a policy of internal promotion—by the time a manager reached an upper management position, he had been working with the actual full cost transfer pricing technique for a long time. Another factor might have been the extraordinary profitability of the company.

Other than reflecting costs as they occur, the actual cost transfer pricing technique, either variable cost or full cost, has little to recommend it. Even the minor advantage of reflecting current costs can be a disadvantage if the costs are subject to fluctuations due to the economies of the volume production or other factors. A more fundamental objection to actual cost is that inefficiencies are simply transferred elsewhere. Thus, poor performance is rewarded the same as good performance. There is also the temptation on the part of the producing division to load the transfer price with extra costs. In the actual cost transfer pricing technique discussed above, the company claimed that loading the transfer price wasn't possible because it was monitored by corporate accounting. In another company that had discontinued actual full cost transfer pricing, however, significant loading of the transfer price had been found. In addition, actual costs cannot be determined before the product is produced, so all transfer pricing is after the fact. Actual costs are difficult to use as effective and efficient transfer prices.

Standard Cost

Of the cost center transfer pricing techniques, standard full cost was the most widely used; it was used by five companies. Four of the five companies used standard full cost, with three of the four using it as their primary technique. The standard costs encountered in the companies in this study actually were budgeted costs. Forecasts for the coming year became standard costs. In essence, the transfer price was based on estimated actual costs because the standard approximated actual.

Standard cost eliminates many disadvantages of actual cost transfer pricing, but full cost is subject to the deficiency described earlier. That is, allocating fixed costs to products obscures profitability decisions.

Standard variable cost approximating actual variable cost, however, could form the basis of a viable transfer pricing technique. Standard costs are more viable than actual costs because they avoid the tendency to load the transfer price. Furthermore, the transfer price is known before the product is produced, thus allowing the transfer price to be accurately included in decision making. There is also the advantage of performance evaluation based on analysis of variances. Standard fixed costs can be handled as period costs rather than product costs.

There are two potential disadvantages of the standard cost transfer pricing technique. First, the cost of the product will not reflect the variances; therefore, the cost is not the true cost, which could affect pricing decisions. Second, standards often are rather loosely determined, even engineered standards. Standard setting involves some guesswork, and standards are easily manipulated. If the standards are forecasts of actual cost, however, the disadvantages of the standard cost transfer pricing technique are somewhat mitigated. On the other hand, using forecasts of actual costs as standards inherently encourages the forecaster to overestimate costs.

Additional Points about Cost Center Transfer Pricing Techniques

There are two points that should be emphasized about cost center transfer pricing techniques. First, the view of this study is a corporate view. That is, the view of transfer pricing is from the top of the organization downward. Hence, the information collected on cost transfer pricing techniques pertains only to those situations where the techniques were used in higher levels of the organization. In fact, all the organizations used cost center transfer pricing techniques someplace in their organization but usually at a very low level. For example, transfers between departments within a single manufacturing plant were at cost, and often transfers between manufacturing facilities in a single profit center were at cost. In most cases, however, transfers between segments higher in the organizational structure were made using a market-based transfer pricing technique. In other words, cost center transfer prices were used widely, but normally at low levels of the organization where performance evaluation emphasized cost control.

The second point is that although cost center transfer pricing techniques are fairly simple to understand, sometimes they are not simple to use. Organizations that use cost center transfer pricing techniques are normally highly vertically integrated; therefore, sometimes it is difficult to determine which division is responsible for various costs.

For example, if Division A runs a special order for Division B, which requires Division A to reschedule production of other products and incur additional costs, who should pay the costs? Division A can argue that the costs would not have been incurred were it not for the special order of Division B. Division B might charge that Division A is inefficient and that it should not have incurred extra charges. In other words, the fate of integrated divisions can be so inextricably intertwined that some costs or variances are actually joint costs. Nevertheless, allocating the joint costs between the divisions is not likely to be a solution. Simply identifying the joint costs would be difficult, as would finding an acceptable basis for allocation. The whole issue would involve negotiation that could lead to the same conflicts as the negotiated transfer pricing technique. In practice, then, cost center transfer pricing techniques are less complicated than most profit center transfer pricing techniques, but their simplicity is somewhat deceiving.

Summary

Chapters 3 and 4 have examined the characteristics, advantages and disadvantages of a number of transfer pricing techniques. All of Chapter 3 and most of Chapter 4 have been devoted to profit center techniques for two reasons. First, usually they are more complicated than cost center techniques, and second, they are more widely used. Seven different profit center transfer pricing techniques were reviewed, all but one of which was used by one or more of the companies in this study. By far the most widely used profit center techniques were market based. Seventy percent of the primary transfer pricing techniques used by companies in this study were market-based techniques, as were 67% of the secondary techniques. This popularity of market-based profit center techniques is a reflection of the current tendency of companies to use highly decentralized profit centers whenever possible.

Nonmarket-based profit center transfer pricing techniques and cost center transfer pricing techniques were not widely used although the former was used more often than the latter. When cost center techniques were used, it was for one of two reasons; either the company was so large that market prices were irrelevant or the intermediate product did not have a reliable market price.

Still unanswered is which transfer pricing technique should be used. The next chapter is devoted exclusively to answering this question.

Notes

1. Harold Bierman, Jr. and Thomas R. Dyckman, *Managerial Cost Accounting,* Macmillan Publishing Co., Inc., New York, 1976, pp. 24-25.
2. For the sake of simplicity, it is assumed that the productive capacity used to produce Product X cannot be used to produce Product W.
3. The idea of utilizing opportunity costs in the form of a lost contribution margin was first introduced by Charles Horngren in "A Contribution Margin Approach to the Analysis of Capacity Utilization," *The Accounting Review,* Vol. 42, No. 3, April 1967, pp. 254-264.
4. Mohamed Onsi, "A Transfer Pricing System Based on Opportunity Cost," *The Accounting Review,* Vol. 65, No. 3, July 1970, pp. 535-543.
5. David Solomons said that one of the companies in his study used the equivalent of a marginal cost transfer price. See Solomons (1965), pp. 183-184.
6. Although not precise, marginal cost can be thought of as the cost of producing the next unit.
7. "Discretionary fixed costs (sometimes called managed or programmed costs) are fixed costs that arise from periodic (usually yearly) appropriation decisions that directly reflect top-management policies . . . Examples are research and development, advertising, sales promotion, donations, management consulting fees and many employee training programs. Conceivably, these costs could be reduced almost entirely for a given year in dire times." Charles T. Horngren, *Cost Accounting: A Managerial Emphasis,* Prentice-Hall, Inc., Englewood Cliffs, N.J., 1977, p. 234.

Chapter 5

Recommendations for Transfer Pricing

With the wide variety of transfer pricing techniques available and few rules for choosing among them, it is difficult for a company to select the best technique. Frequently a company finds that several transfer pricing techniques appear to be suited to its circumstances. As a result, the decision to use a particular technique can be influenced by factors separate from the actual process and impact of transfer pricing. For example, the decision may be influenced by a division manager's preference for a certain technique or staff recommendations based on insufficient understanding of the various techniques under consideration.

The selection of a transfer pricing technique should not be arbitrary. Although there may appear to be several techniques suited to a company's circumstances, one will be better than the others. A procedure is needed that will guide the management of a company when selecting the transfer pricing technique.

Criteria Used For Evaluating the Results of the General Rule

Three criteria should be fulfilled by a transfer pricing technique in order for it to be suited to an organization. The technique should (1) promote profit maximization, (2) enhance performance evaluation, and (3) be understood easily. We discussed the first two criteria in Chapter 2. They are based on the need for consistency between the transfer pricing technique and the objectives of the management control process. The third criterion is simply a matter of practicality. Business managers do not have the time to learn complicated processes.

The first criterion for selecting a transfer pricing technique is that it should lead to profit maximization in *almost all* instances. Simply noting a few circumstances under which profit will not be maximized with a particular transfer pricing technique is not sufficient reason for rejecting the technique. Profit maximization, although important, is an ill-defined, largely unmeasurable concept that considers only what can be translated into dollars. Profit maximization in *most* instances is a sufficient criterion for a transfer pricing technique, but to insist that it occur in all instances is a utopian desire that has little relevance to actual business practice.

Because performance evaluation of either a profit or a cost center is a crucial aspect of the management control process, the second criterion is that the transfer pricing technique selected should enhance, not impede, the evaluation. For example, if profit centers are used with a transfer pricing technique such as cost-plus, an artificial profit is created, resulting in a pseudo-profit center. Evaluation of the performance of a pseudo-profit center on a profit basis is almost meaningless because the extent of the profit or loss depends on the transfer pricing technique. If the prevailing market price technique is used with profit centers, however, performance evaluation will not be impeded.

The third criterion is that the transfer pricing technique selected must be as simple as possible. Business managers have little time or desire to learn complicated procedures, and a transfer pricing technique that is not simple will not be well understood so may be challenged as unfair. A simple technique, assuming it fulfills the first two criteria, will be accepted more readily than a complicated one.

Thus, three criteria should be used to select a transfer pricing technique. The technique selected by the general rule should

1. Lead to profit maximization in *almost all* instances,
2. Enhance performance evaluation, and
3. Be understood easily.

In addition, the transfer pricing technique selected should be as consistent as possible with management's philosophy of decentralization although there will be occasions where this philosophy will be difficult to realize.

The General Rule for Selecting Transfer Pricing Techniques

Almost everyone would agree that the most useful transfer pricing technique is one that is suitable for all situations, leads to profit maximization in every instance, and is simple. Unfortunately, no such transfer pricing technique exists. Industries are too diverse, products too different, and circumstances too dissimilar for a single all-encompassing transfer pricing technique.

Even though an all-encompassing transfer pricing technique does not exist, there is a general rule that will guide a company toward the best transfer pricing technique for its situation. *The general transfer pricing rule is that the transfer price should equal the standard variable cost (SVC) plus the contribution margin per unit on the outside sale given up by the company when a segment sells internally. The contribution margin given up, referred to hereafter as the lost contribution margin (LCM), is the difference between the external market price (MP) of the product sold internally and its standard variable cost. This difference contributes to fixed cost, profit, and any variances from standard. If the product does not have a market price and a suitable substitute cannot be found, the lost contribution margin is zero.*

The general transfer pricing rule can be expressed more succinctly:

The transfer price equals the standard variable cost plus the lost contribution margin

or

$$TP = SVC + LCM.$$

Standard variable cost is used for cost control purposes. A number of companies that participated in the present study had in the past used actual cost (variable or full) as part of the transfer price, but this procedure caused a conflict between the supplying and receiving divisions. For example, one company in the present study used actual full cost to transfer about 25% of a division's product. As expected, the transfer price fluctuated with changes in cost. The receiving division complained vigorously that the supplying division was not producing efficiently because the supplying division knew it could transfer its inefficiencies to the receiving division. The argument was never resolved. Finally, the company changed to a market-based transfer pricing technique.

In spite of the scientific aura that surrounds standard cost, there is little that is scientific about it. The measurement process to establish the standards is somewhat scientific, but even before the standards are established, management must decide whether the standards will be difficult to attain, easy to attain, or somewhere in between. The decision is subjective. Furthermore, the decision can be changed and standards manipulated. Therefore, whenever standard cost is used as part of the transfer price, one must take care in determining the level of the standards.

As visualized here, standard variable cost refers to expected results;

that is, the standards are developed at the beginning of each year to approximate actual costs. Other definitions of standards can be used, however, in which case it must be remembered that standard cost and actual cost may be considerably different.

Fixed costs are not included as part of the transfer price. The reasons for excluding fixed costs were discussed in detail in Chapter 4 under cost center transfer pricing techniques. The effect of this exclusion will become apparent as the application of the general rule is discussed.

The second part of the general transfer pricing rule, the lost contribution margin, is more often known as the opportunity cost. Lost contribu-

---

EXHIBIT 5-1

Profit Maximizing with Contribution Margins

Assume that Division A manufactures a product with a standard variable cost of $5. Division A can sell the product externally for $8, or it can sell the product to Division B. Division B further processes the product at a standard variable cost of $4 and sells the product externally for $14.[1]

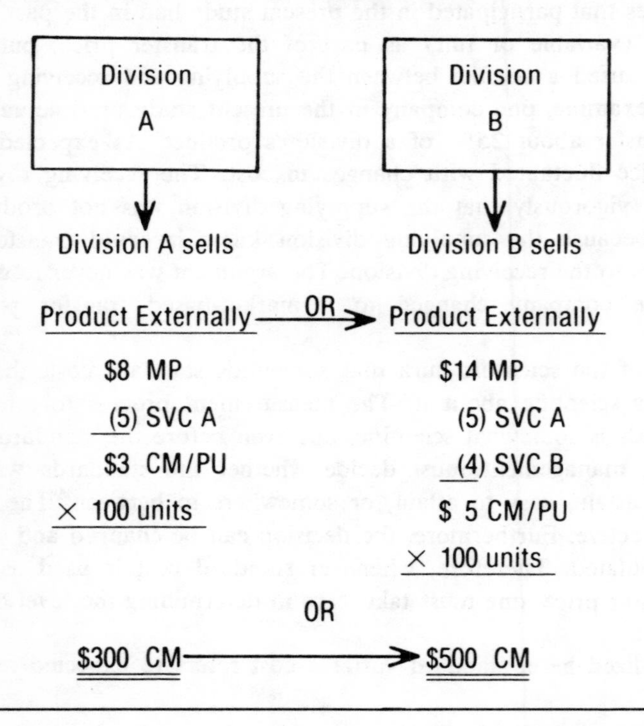

---

tion margin can be defined as the contribution given up by the company when it chooses one course of action over another. For example, if the company can sell a product externally for $8 when the standard variable cost is $5, the lost contribution margin is $3 if the company decides to sell the product internally for $5. Of course, the company will wish to sell the product internally rather than externally only if the receiving division can increase the contribution margin to greater than $3. This can be illustrated easily. See Exhibit 5-1.

If Division A sells the product externally, Division A and the company receive a contribution margin (CM) of $300. If Division A transfers the product to Division B and Division B sells the product externally, Division B and the company receive a contribution margin of $500 rather than $300. In other words, the company should sacrifice the $3 contribution margin per unit in favor of the $5 contribution margin per unit. The lost contribution margin is $3. Applying the general rule to this illustration, the transfer price per unit is $8 (SVC + LCM or $5 + $3 = $8), the market price. The effect of the transfer price on both divisions and the company is shown in Exhibit 5-2.

EXHIBIT 5-2
The General Rule Applied to Exhibit 5-1

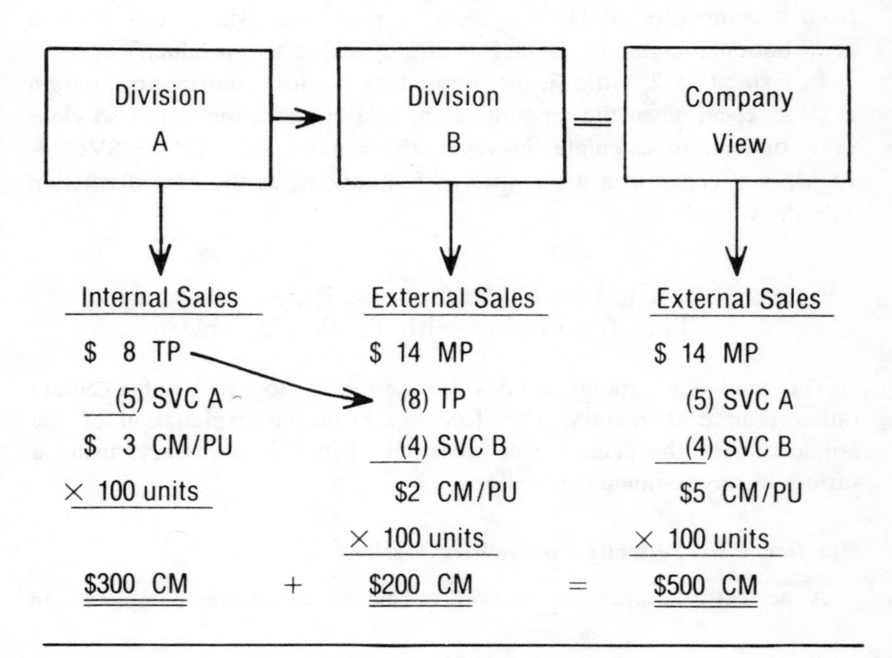

Division A receives the same contribution margin it would receive if the product were sold externally. Division B buys from Division A and adds a contribution margin of $2 to each unit, bringing the contribution margin per unit to $5 for the company.

Adding the lost contribution margin to the standard variable cost leads to profit maximization. If the contribution margin from the alternative the company *did not* select (in the example, Division A sells externally) were greater than the contribution margin the company receives from the alternative it *did* select (transferring the product to Division B to earn a $5 CM/PU), Division A would not transfer to Division B, and the company still would achieve maximum profit. For example, suppose the external market price for Division A is $11 rather than $8. Division A and the company will have a contribution margin of $6 ($11 – $5 = $6) if Division A sells the product externally but only $5 if it sells the product internally (the same $5 it had before). The transfer price will be $11 ($5 + $6 = $11). This transfer price will lead to a negative contribution margin for Division B, so no transfers will occur. This situation is shown in Exhibit 5-3.

In this situation it is better for the company if Division A sells externally rather than to Division B. The transfer price of $11 prevents Division B from buying from Division A because if it does so, its contribution margin is ($1). If Division B cannot buy the product from a competitor of Division A at a price that will give a positive contribution margin, Division B will stop using the product.[2]

In Exhibits 5-2 and 5-3, the amount of the lost contribution margin is clear. Even when the amount of the lost contribution is not so clear or is difficult to calculate, however, the general rule, TP = SVC + LCM, is effective in a wide variety of situations, as the next discussion will show.

The Use of the General Rule for Transfer Pricing with Profit Centers

The tendency among today's businesses is to use profit centers rather than cost centers. Therefore, an extensive explanation of the application of the general rule to profit centers is necessary, using a variety of environmental situations.

Situation #1—Perfectly Competitive Markets

A perfectly competitive market is one in which the company can

EXHIBIT 5-3

The General Rule Applied with an $11 External Market Price

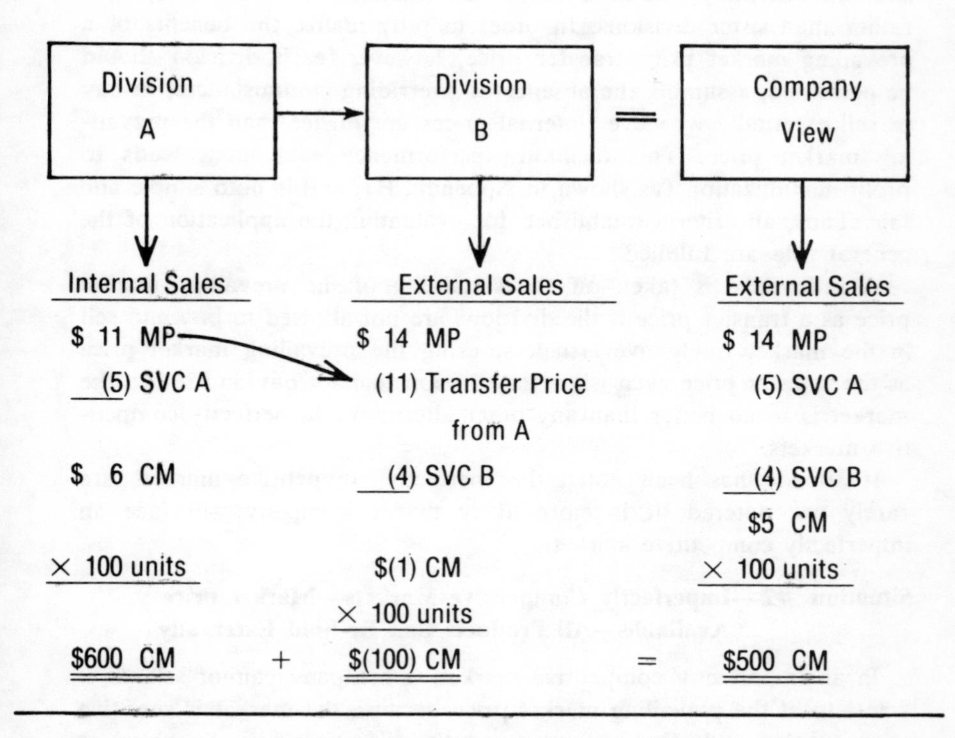

sell all it produces at the current market price. In the business environment, perfectly competitive markets are rare, particularly for large companies. Nevertheless, showing the application of the general rule to perfectly competitive markets lays the foundation for understanding the more complex application of the rule to imperfectly competitive markets discussed in Situation #2.

The examples in Exhibits 5-2 and 5-3 implicitly assume that the market is perfectly competitive because they assume that if Division B does not buy from Division A, Division A can sell its products externally at the prevailing market price. Furthermore, Division A's sales in the market do not affect the prevailing market price.

In both Exhibits 5-2 and 5-3, the general rule, SVC + LCM, was applied to determine the transfer price, and in both illustrations the general rule led to the transfer price equaling the prevailing market price. In perfectly competitive markets, the prevailing market price is the best transfer price. Because the divisions can act as independent businesses, performance evaluation is enhanced. The divisions can buy and sell internally just as if they were trading with other companies rather than sister divisions. In order to fully realize the benefits of a prevailing market price transfer price, however, each division should be permitted, assuming the absence of overriding circumstances, to buy or sell externally whenever internal prices are higher than the prevailing market price. This facilitates performance evaluation, leads to profit maximization (as shown in Appendix B), and is both simple and fair. Thus, all criteria established for evaluating the application of the general rule are fulfilled.

A little edge is taken off the suitability of the prevailing market price as a transfer price if the divisions are not allowed to buy and sell in the market freely. Nevertheless, using the prevailing market price as the transfer price even when the divisions cannot buy and sell in the market is much better than any other alternative in perfectly competitive markets.

It already has been noted that perfectly competitive markets are rarely encountered; it is more likely that a company will face an imperfectly competitive market.

Situation #2—Imperfectly Competitive Markets—Market Price Available—All Products Can Be Sold Externally

In an imperfectly competitive market, a company cannot sell all it wants to at the prevailing market price because the market is sensitive to quantities sold. For example, quantity discounts may be given or special terms relating to delivery, payment, service, and warranty may be extended to the buyer.

Imperfectly competitive markets prevailed strongly for one of the companies in our study. In this company one division purchased and refined metals. Although the division could sell the refined metal in the market, it could not do so at the prices quoted daily in *The Wall Street Journal* because the price was sensitive to quantities sold. However, all the product of the refining division was sold internally to other divisions at the market price (slightly adjusted) quoted in *The Wall Street Journal*. As a result of internal sales, the refining division was extraordinarily profitable, and the division manager argued loudly and frequently for expansion of his division. It seemed logical that if the refining division were allowed to expand production for external sale, the company could increase profits significantly. The division manager even suggested shutting down the other divisions and diverting all resources to the refining division. Unfortunately the refining division manager ignored the fact that his division faced an imperfectly competitive market.

How can the transfer price be determined in an imperfectly competitive market? The answer is not easy and depends upon the degree of market imperfection. Three degrees of market imperfection will be examined: slightly imperfectly competitive, moderately imperfectly competitive, and significantly imperfectly competitive.

Slightly Imperfectly Competitive Markets

A slightly imperfectly competitive market is characterized by small quantity discounts, special payment terms, or other trade considerations. Special inducements are necessary for a company to sell all its production, but by offering these special inducements, the company is able to sell externally all it can produce. In addition, the company may have selling expenses and bad debt expense associated with external sales.

These items can be referred to as identifiable and quantifiable imperfections in the market, and they must be taken into consideration when the transfer price is determined, or the company will make some decisions that do not lead to profit maximization. For example, in Exhibit 5-3 the transfer price was set at the prevailing market price of $11 (SVC + LCM = MP or $5 + $6 = $11). Suppose, however, that the saving to Division A of selling internally is $2 per unit sold because Division A avoids selling expenses, bad debt expense, and warranty expense. This amount, although admittedly rather high, is sufficient for illustration purposes. The situation would be as shown in Exhibit 5-4 (page 84) if the transfer price is set at the prevailing market price.

From the viewpoint of the company, the profit maximizing decision is to sell internally to Division B for a company contribution margin of $700. Division B will not buy from Division A, however, when the prevailing market price is the transfer price because this would give Division B a $1 per unit negative contribution.[3] The solution is to lower the transfer price by subtracting from the SVC the amount of cost saved by selling internally, thus deriving an adjusted market price. Alternatively, the adjusted market price could be determined by subtracting the cost savings from the prevailing market price.

For example, in Exhibit 5-4 the contribution margin for external sales is $6 ($11 market price – $5 SVC-A). Thus, $6 is the lost contribution margin. The $5 SVC-A would be adjusted downward to $3 to reflect the $2 cost savings from selling internally. The general rule

EXHIBIT 5-4
Using an Unadjusted Prevailing Market Price

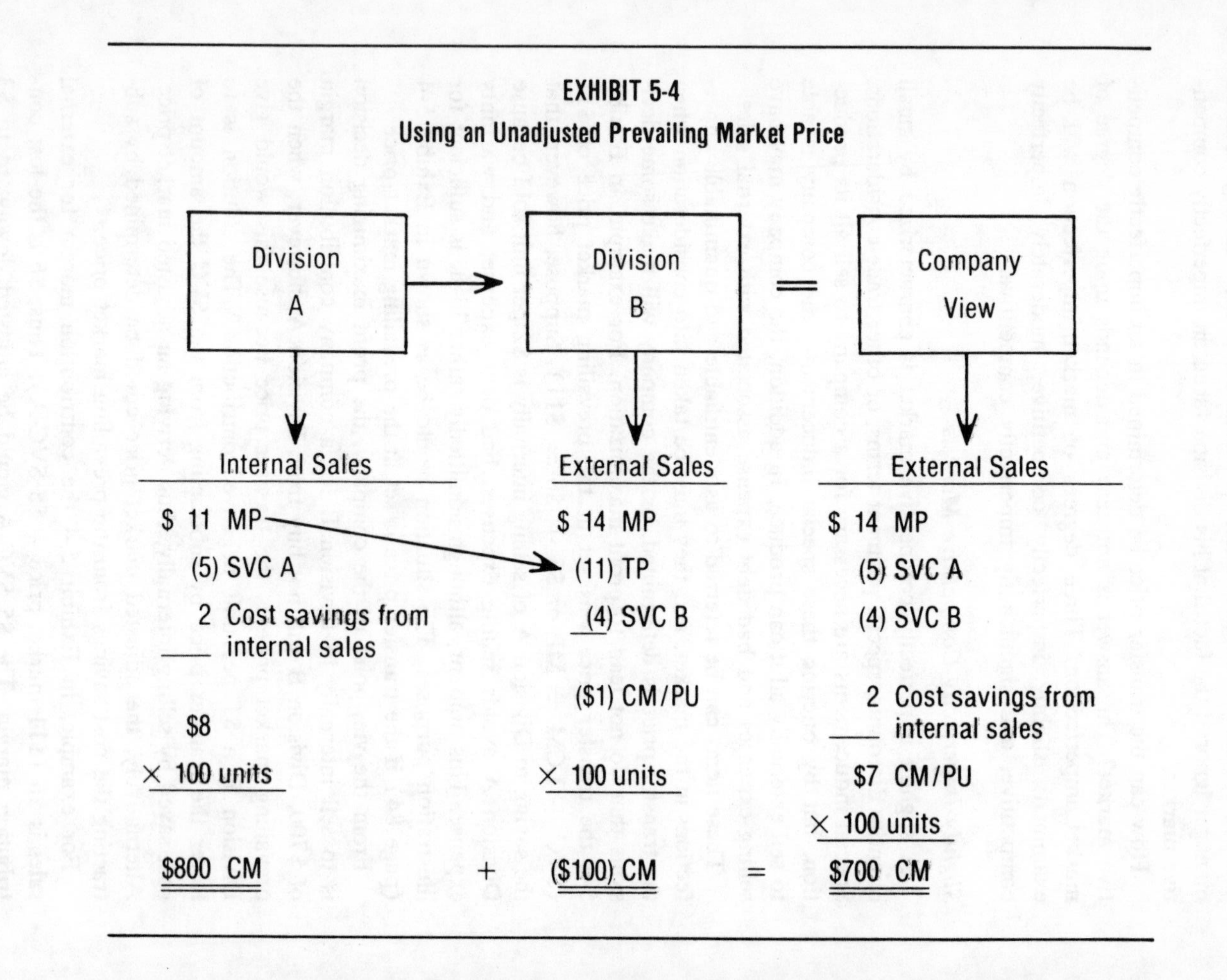

EXHIBIT 5-5

Using the Adjusted Market Price

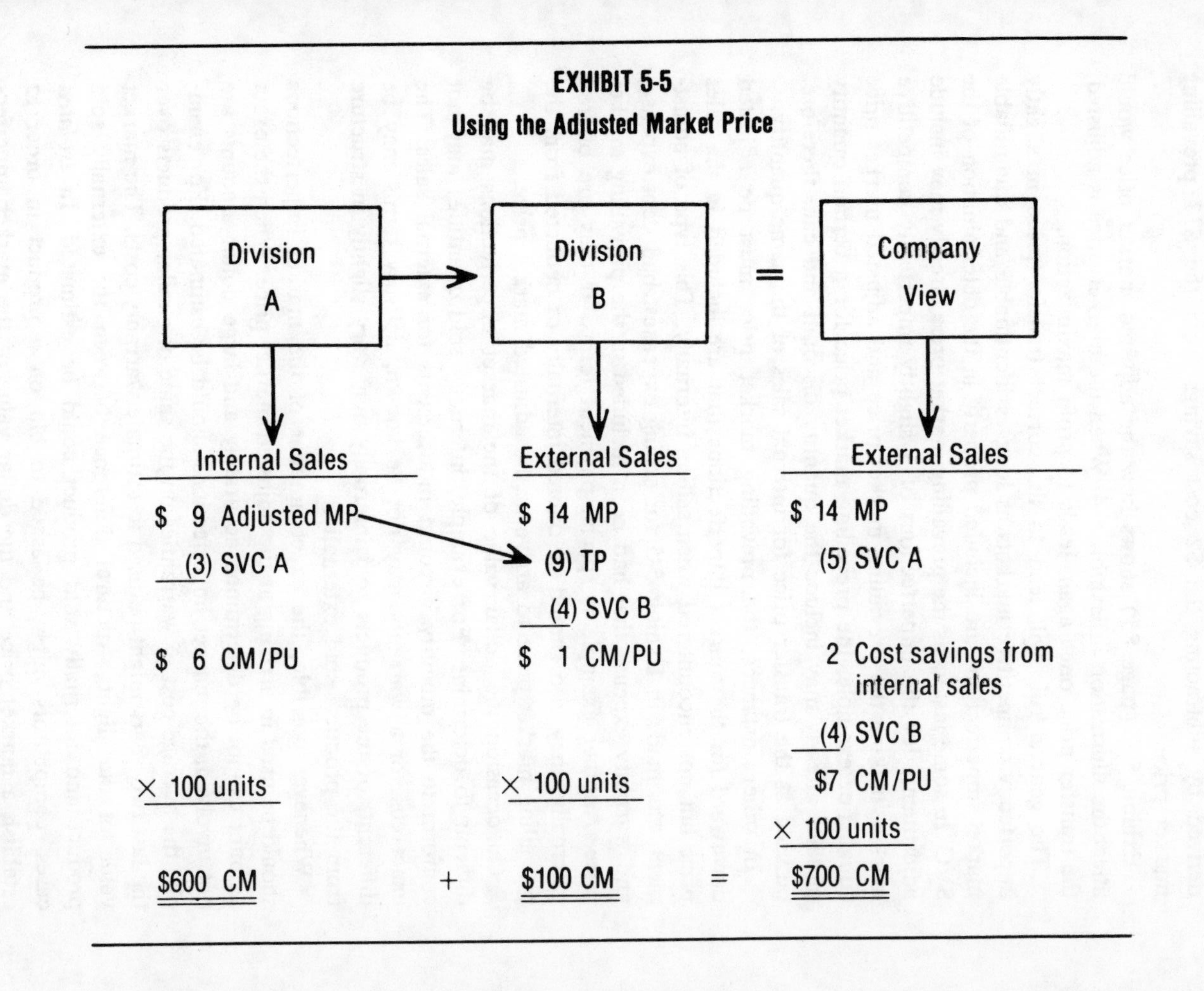

gives a transfer price of $9 (SVC + LCM = $3 + $6 = $9). The $9 transfer price is the adjusted market price, which could have been derived by subtracting the $2 cost savings from the $11 prevailing market price.

Exhibit 5-5 (page 85) shows how the adjusted market price would affect the illustration in Exhibit 5-4. When the market price is adjusted, the transfer price once again leads to profit maximization.

The general rule will lead to the correct transfer price in slightly imperfectly competitive markets as long as identifiable and quantifiable market imperfections are included properly in the determination of the SVC. In some instances the prevailing market price already may include adjustments for the imperfections of a slightly imperfectly competitive market, making the prevailing market price and adjusted market price equal. For example, the prevailing market price for a certain quantity of sales already may include the quantity discount and can, therefore, be used as the transfer price for internal sales of the same quantity.

In other instances, the prevailing market price must be adjusted downward for the market imperfections that are included in the sales price but not encountered when selling internally. This type of adjustment was made in Exhibit 5-5 for selling expenses, bad debt expense, and warranty expense that had been included in the prevailing market price. Another example is special payment terms. If they are offered externally, they also should be offered internally or deducted from the prevailing market price to arrive at the adjusted market price.

On occasion the dollar value of the market imperfections may be difficult to determine. For example, internally sold quantities may not conform to the quantity discount inducements for external sales. The exact cost of a warranty may not be known, delivery terms may be different, or the products sold internally may vary slightly in structure from the products sold externally.

Whenever possible, the exact amount of the market imperfections should be used in arriving at the adjusted market price. When the exact amount cannot be determined accurately and large dollar amounts are not involved, the market imperfections should be estimated. For example, the average cost of warranties on the same or similar products over the last two years might be used to estimate warranty costs. The market value of the slight structural difference between the externally sold product and internally sold product could be estimated. In *isolated* cases, competitors might be asked to bid on a product in order to establish a market price and the dollar value of the market imperfections. As long as the estimates are fairly close to the true amounts, little harm will be done and the second criterion, profit maximization in almost all instances, will be fulfilled. Of course, the more the estimates stray from the true amounts, the more the company will fail to maximize profit.

Some companies that adhere to a corporate philosophy of strict divisional autonomy may wish to leave the adjustment of the market price open to negotiation. A negotiated adjustment probably would be close to a company-determined adjustment and therefore would not be harmful to the company. The supplying division manager and receiving division manager negotiate, guided by the knowledge that the prevailing market price is too high for transfer pricing. It is true that in this process negotiation skills will play a role in determining the deductions from the prevailing market price. As long as the dollar value involved is small, however, this is a trivial consequence. Information will be available to both managers that will guide them in the negotiation process. It is extremely unlikely that one manager will so overwhelm the other that performance evaluation will be very much affected. Thus, even with a negotiation process determining the deduction from the prevailing market price, the transfer price will be restricted to a fairly narrow range.

If large dollar amounts are involved, however, the inducement should not be estimated or negotiated. The company would not be facing a slightly imperfectly competitive market and would be in danger of straying from realistic market prices to such an extent that performance evaluation might be misleading and profit maximization might not occur. Thus, two of the three criteria for evaluating the transfer pricing technique selected would be significantly violated. Only if the dollar values are small should the company estimate the value of the market imperfections.

Many companies face slightly imperfectly competitive markets. In such a market the adjusted market price, which is equal to SVC plus LCM, should be used as the transfer price although the transfer price can be determined more efficiently by subtracting identifiable and quantifiable market imperfections from the prevailing market price if the imperfections have not already been subtracted. When the dollar amounts involved are small, the market imperfections can be estimated or negotiated. A transfer price determined in this manner will fulfill the three criteria for evaluating the general rule.

Moderately Imperfectly Competitive Markets

The difference between a slightly imperfectly competitive market and a moderately imperfectly competitive market is that in the latter, increased quantities of products sold externally are caused by declines in the price per unit. In other words, in a moderately imperfectly competitive market, the company faces a downward sloping demand curve.[4] In this situation it is very difficult to determine the lost contribution margin. The reasons for the difficulty are shown in Exhibit 5-6.

As Exhibit 5-6 shows, Division B will not buy from Division A or anyone else when the prevailing market price is $11. As a consequence, Division A now must sell the 100 units externally. However, since the market is moderately imperfectly competitive, Division A finds that it must lower the price to $9 per unit in order to sell 200 units. The result is shown in Exhibit 5-7 (page 90).

The analysis in Exhibit 5-7 shows that using the prevailing market price of $11 as the transfer price was incorrect. The $11 transfer price led Division B to stop using the product it purchased from Division A, thereby lowering the contribution margin for the company.

It is clear from Exhibit 5-7 that in order to achieve profit maximization, the transfer price should be lower than $11. This process can be accomplished with a two-tiered transfer pricing technique, but the company, not the divisions, must determine the optimal level of production[5] and the amount of internal and external sales because the optimal level of production and profit depends upon Divisions A and B together. Without a joint effort, Division A might increase its profits at the expense of the company by selling externally part of the products needed by Division B. Assuming that the company does set the level of production and internal sales, the analysis is as shown in Exhibit 5-8 (page 91).

The transfer price in Exhibit 5-8 is $7 (SVC + LCM = $5 + $2 = $7). The LCM is composed of two parts. The first part is the contribution foregone of $4 when the 100 units are sold internally ($9 expected sales price – $5 standard variable cost). The second part is the $2 saved ($11 current sales price – $9 expected sales price) on the units now sold externally by selling the other 100 units internally. Thus, the transfer price is $5 SVC + [$4 – $2] LCM = $7. The company has returned to the contribution margin of $1,100 and the two-tiered technique has led to profit maximization.

In spite of the technical correctness of the analysis in Exhibit 5-8, however, a two-tiered transfer pricing technique is probably not a very useful solution to transfer pricing in a moderately imperfectly competitive market. Except under unusual conditions, it would at best be difficult to determine the market price of the total production (internal and external sales) because the internal sales actually are not sold externally. The prevailing market price for internal sales that could

EXHIBIT 5-6

Moderately Imperfectly Competitive Markets

Shown below is the illustration used in Exhibit 5-3. In this illustration, a transfer price of SVC + LCM = MP or \$5 + \$6 = S11 led to the correct decisions of Division A, which refines metals, to sell its product externally rather than to Division B. Here the illustration is changed slightly because 200 units are assumed, 100 sold externally and 100 sold internally.

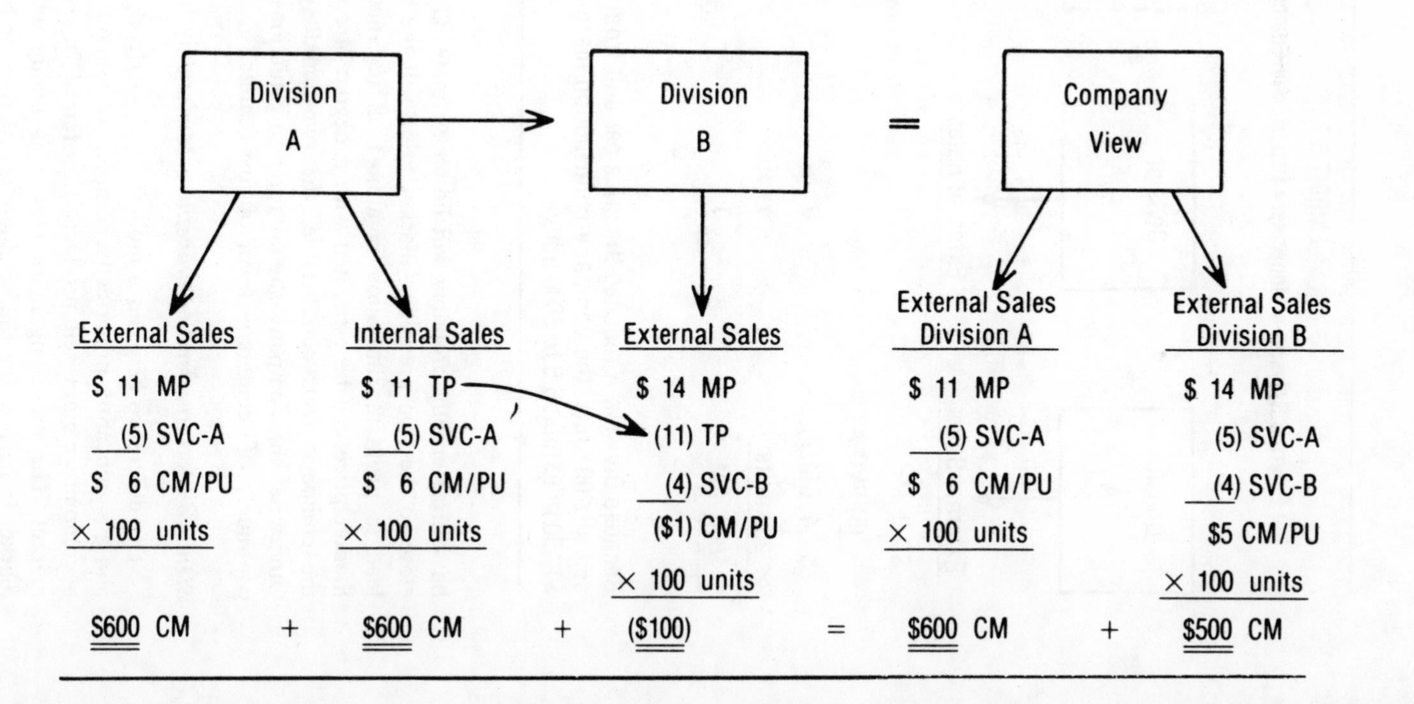

EXHIBIT 5-7

External Sales in a Moderately Imperfectly Competitive Market

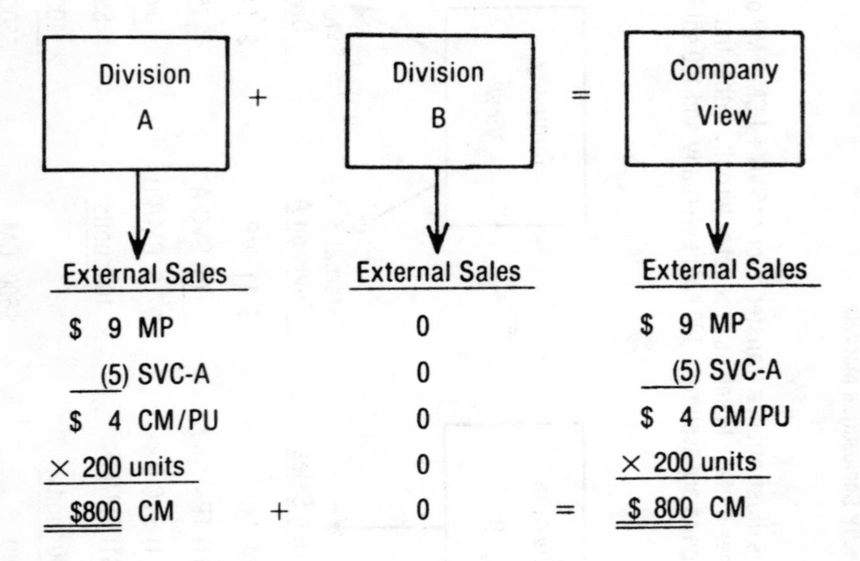

Because Division A reduced the price per unit from $11 to $9 in order to sell all 200 units, the company contribution margin has declined from $1,100 in Exhibit 5-6 to $800 above.

be sold externally probably will be an estimate. Only if the estimate is close to the true prevailing market price will the two-tiered technique lead to profit maximization in almost all instances. If the prevailing market price can be estimated with a degree of confidence with which the company feels comfortable, the two-tiered system can be used. Otherwise, the company should refer to Situations #3 or #4 or discontinue profit centers in favor of cost centers.

Significantly Imperfectly Competitive Markets

The difference between a moderately imperfectly competitive market and a significantly imperfectly competitive market is that in the latter, a company cannot sell products transferred internally in an external market. The prevailing market price is highly unreliable because the market is narrow for the products transferred or because the company

EXHIBIT 5-8

Two-Tiered Transfer Pricing Technique

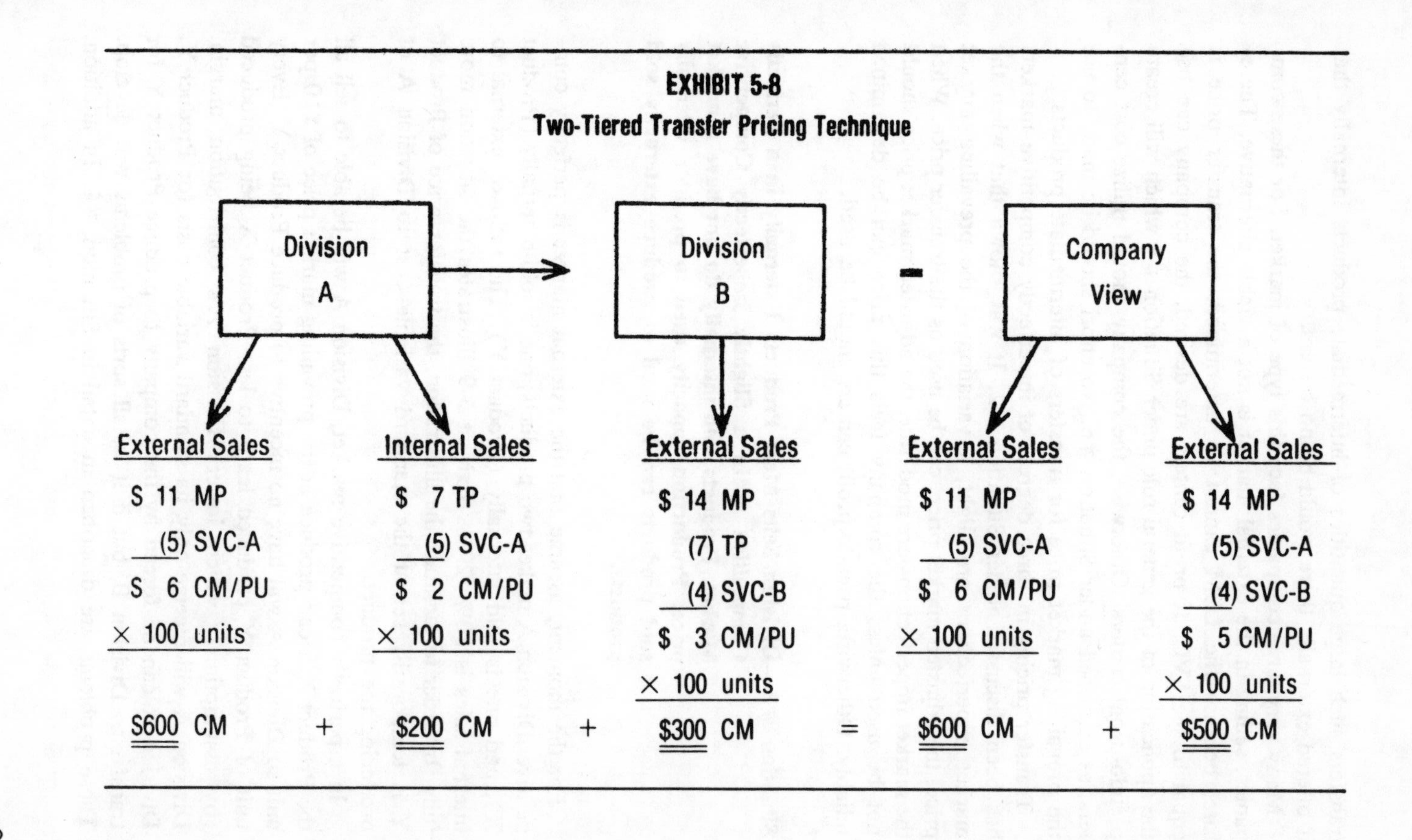

transfers such large quantities of intermediate products internally that if offered externally there would be no buyers.

Many very large companies face this type of market. For these companies, selling in the external market is not a viable alternative. Therefore, because the LCM cannot be determined, the transfer price is equal to the SVC. If profit centers are desired, the company can use the application of the general rule under Situation #4 which will create pseudo-profit centers. Otherwise, the company should utilize cost centers, as described under Situation #6. No effort should be made to use the prevailing market price for transfers of intermediate products.

Transfer pricing in three degrees of imperfectly competitive markets has been discussed under Situation #2. It was shown that when the market imperfections are slight, a variation of the prevailing market price, the adjusted market price, can be used as the transfer price. When the market imperfections are moderate, the adjusted market price should not be used unless the company feels this price can be determined reliably. Otherwise, pseudo-profit centers should be used.

Situation #3—Division Sells Most Products Externally in a Perfectly Competitive or in a Slightly Imperfectly Competitive Market. Products sold internally do not have a market price. Production capacity used to produce internally sold products can be used to produce externally sold products.

For the moment, assume that the external market is perfectly competitive. Division A makes two products; one is sold externally (Product X), and one is sold internally (Product Y). The ratio of external to internal sales is 80%/20%. Exhibit 5-9 illustrates the situation more fully. In order to facilitate the illustration, the transfer price of Product Y is temporarily set at the standard variable cost to Division A of producing the product.

In a perfectly competitive market, Division A will be able to sell all the Product X it can produce at the prevailing market price of $10 per unit so Division A will have no incentive to produce Product Y. Every unit of Product Y produced leads to less Product X being produced (by assumption), which lowers Division A's contribution margin. Division A will receive only its standard variable costs for Product Y. Division A can be forced by the company to produce Product Y for transfer to Division B, but if it is, all sorts of problems will develop. These problems are described in detail in Situation #4. In addition,

EXHIBIT 5-9

Transfer Pricing at the SVC in a Profit Center

Division A → Division B = Company View

Division A: External Sales Product X		Division A: Internal Sales Product Y		Division B: External Sales Product Y		Company View: External Sales Product X		Company View: External Sales Product Y
				$ 14 MP				
$10 MP		$5 TP →		(5) TP		$10 MP		$ 14 MP
(6) SVC-A		(5) SVC-A		(4) SVC-B		(6) SVC-A		(5) SVC-A
$ 4 CM/PU		$0 CM/PU		$ 5 CM/PU				(4) SVC-B
× 160 units		× 40 units		× 40 units		$ 4 CM/PU	+	$ 5 CM/PU
						× 160 units		× 40 units
$640 CM	+	$0 CM	+	$200 CM	=	$640 CM	+	$200 CM

forcing Division A to produce Product Y will reduce Division A's autonomy.

The dilemma is solved by using a phantom market price. The transfer price that should be used is covered by the general rule, TP= SVC + LCM, with the LCM equal to the contribution margin of Product X since Product X must be sacrificed in order to produce Product Y. The lost contribution margin equals $4 per unit. This situation is illustrated in Exhibit 5-10.

Exhibit 5-10 shows that at a transfer price of $9 (TP = SVC + LCM = $5 + $4 = $9), Division B will buy from Division A, which leads to a contribution margin for the company of $5 per unit on Product Y. Division A has an incentive to supply Division B with all the Product Y Division B needs because Division A receives a contribution margin of $4 per unit which is equal to its other opportunity, selling Product X.

In essence, Divisions A and B share the contribution margin of Product Y by allowing Division A to earn the same contribution margin on Product Y that it would have earned on Product X if Product X had been produced with the productive capacity used to produce Product Y. Thus, a phantom market price is created for Product Y to use as a transfer price.

The more important question is how to set the transfer price when Product X is sold in an imperfectly competitive market, as is likely to be the case. Because the contribution margin of Product X determines the transfer price of Product Y, the adjusted market price of Product X under imperfectly competitive market conditions is needed. This price would be determined in a manner identical to that described under Situation #2 for slightly imperfectly competitive markets. Once the adjusted market price of Product X is determined, the contribution margin, and hence the transfer price of Product Y, can be calculated. If the market for Product X is more than slightly imperfectly competitive, a pseudo-profit center or cost center should be used for the division.

To summarize, when the product sold internally does not have a market price but the majority of the products produced by the supplying division do have a market price, the general rule, TP = SVC + LCM, is used to determine the transfer price. The LCM is the contribution margin not earned on products that could be produced and sold externally if products were not produced for internal sale. This statement assumes that the productive facilities used to produce the internally sold products can be used to produce the externally sold products.

EXHIBIT 5-10

The Phantom Market Price as a Transfer Price

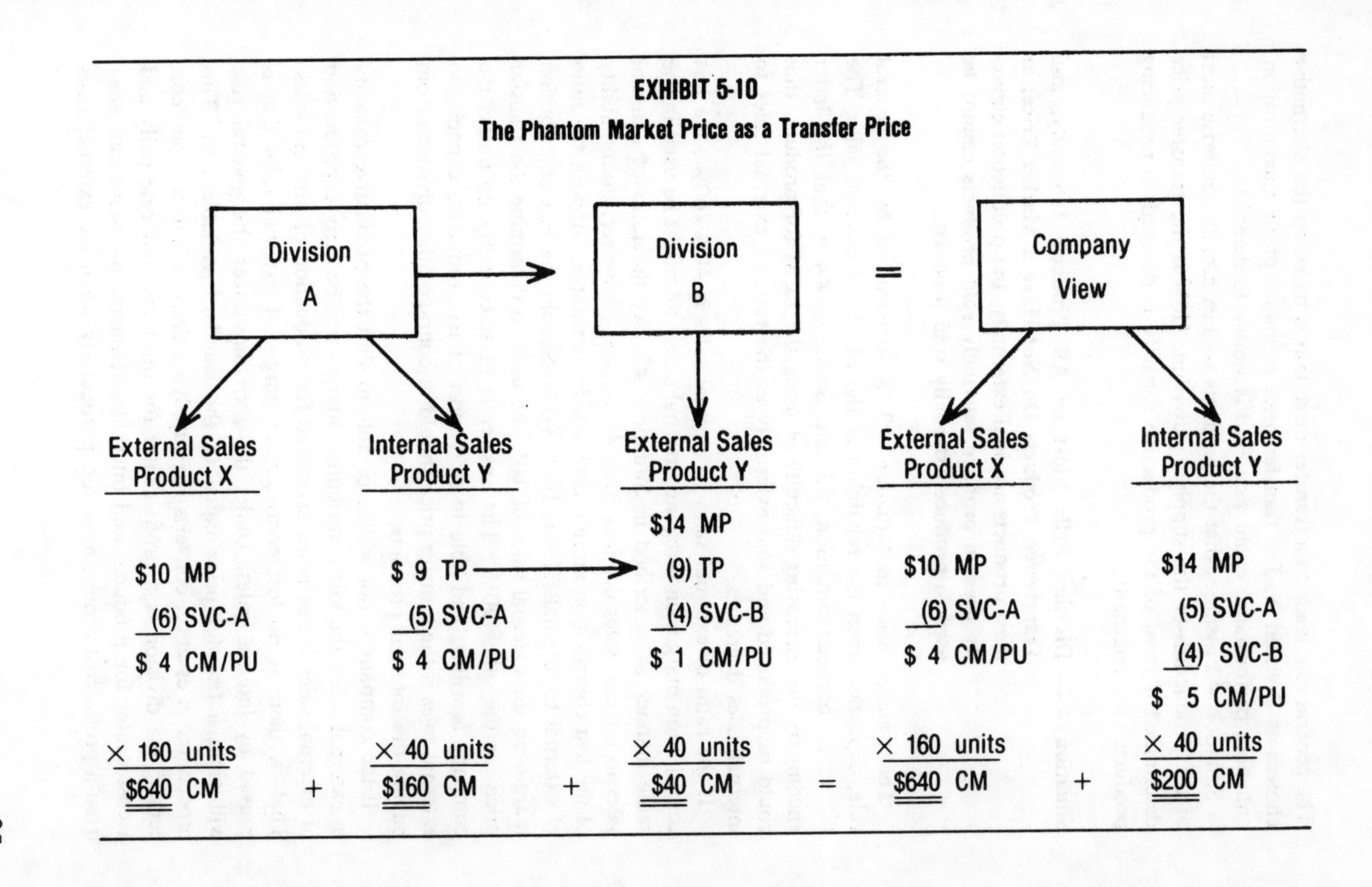

The general rule leads to a transfer price that is based on the alternative choices of Division A. The transfer price promotes profit maximization, enhances performance evaluation, and is simple to determine.

Situation #3 assumes that the products sold externally comprise most of the production of the supplying division. How is the transfer price determined if most of the productive capacity is devoted to producing products sold internally?

Situation #4—Division Sells Most or All Products Internally, and Transferred Products Do Not Have a Market Price; or most products are sold externally, but production capacity used to produce internally sold products cannot be used to produce externally sold products.

The transfer price in Situation #3, as determined by the general rule, depended upon the reliability of the LCM for external sales. The difference between Situation #3 and Situation #4 is that the latter encounters the increasing difficulty of using the LCM for products that could be produced and sold externally as the ratio of external sales to internal sales decreases.

If the ratio of external sales to internal sales is 40%/60%, the lost contribution margin on foregone external sales still might be used in the same manner as described in Situation #3. As the ratio of external sales to internal sales declines from 40%/60%, however, the reliability of the lost contribution margin declines. For example, suppose the ratio of external to internal sales is 10%/90%. Should the lost contribution margin on the external sales of 10% be used to determine the transfer price for the other 90%? The answer is most certainly no unless the company is willing and able to shift most of its productive capacity to external sales if the transfer price should discourage other divisions from buying the internal products.

If the company is not willing or able to shift the productive capacity to external sales, the lost contribution margin will be zero as production of external sales is not being sacrificed for production of internal sales. That is, there is no lost contribution margin of external sales that is caused by internal sales. Under these circumstances the general rule will yield a transfer price equal to the standard variable cost. This procedure, in essence, converts the supplying division into a profit/cost center; the division is a profit center for products sold externally and a cost center for products sold internally. Difficult problems can arise from a profit/cost center, however, particularly when the external sales are fairly high, say over 25-30%. The principal problem is described by the experience of one of the companies in this study.

> All the divisions in the company were profit centers, and management tended to emphasize profits in its evaluation of divisional performance.
>
> Division A was a single large facility that had been constructed with extra capacity to supply Division B. During a year, Division A would sell about three-fourths of its output externally at the prevailing market price and transfer one-fourth internally at actual full cost. Although Division A was not the sole source of Division B's input, it was a significant source.
>
> Three severe problems arose as a result of the procedures used, the most important of which could not be resolved without a change in the transfer pricing technique. The first problem, and the most important one, centered around Division A's being a partly profit, partly cost center. During those months that Division A could find sufficient external customers for more than three-fourths of its product, Division A tended to short Division B or delay transfers. On the other hand, during the months that Division A could not sell three-fourths of its product externally, Division B was swamped with transferred products. Thus, Division B had a very unreliable supply source. The profit incentive was so great that even corporate headquarters could not control the flow from Division A to Division B.
>
> The second problem, which could have been controlled with standard costs, was that since the transfers were at actual cost, the costs transferred to Division B tended to be fairly high. Any actual cost that Division A could transfer to Division B improved Division A's profit.
>
> The third problem, which also could have been cured with the use of standard costs, was that because actual cost was transferred to Division B, the Division B manager did not know the transfer price until after Division A closed its books. The cost was transferred monthly.
>
> There was constant battle between the Division A and Division B managers, but the entire problem evaporated when the president of the company allowed transfers from Division A to Division B at the prevailing market price.

When Division A was a profit/cost center with a profit orientation, the transfers to Division B were of low priority to Division A. When the transfers were at the prevailing market price, Division A was indifferent to selling externally or transferring to Division B because the profit was the same. Division A still had a tendency, during periods of slow external sales, to transfer excess products to Division B, but this problem was controlled by proper planning.

To avoid the problem of misdirected motivation caused by a profit/cost center, the center needs to be converted to a total profit center or a total cost center. Conversion to a total cost center would be simple. Conversion to a total profit center would not be very difficult under certain conditions, the principal condition being that the division producing the product and the division selling the product form a single profit center with respect to the product or products involved. The contribution margin transfer pricing technique could be used to convert a profit/cost center into a total profit center. The procedures involved are described in detail in Chapter 3.

When *all* products produced are sold internally, the contribution margin technique can be used to convert a cost center into a pseudo-profit center. Two large companies in the present study used this technique for all products. In one of the companies the profit from the final sale of the product was allocated first between the manufacturing division and the selling division. The manufacturing division further allocated its share of the contribution margin among a large number of smaller manufacturing divisions. All allocations were based on standard full cost. Thus, in this vertically integrated company, the final profit was allocated all the way back to the smallest manufacturing facilities, and pseudo-profit centers were created all the way down the company's hierarchy.

The circumstances under which the contribution margin technique can be used to convert a cost center into a profit center or a profit/cost center into a profit center are fairly restrictive. First, there should be few end products or the allocation process becomes too complicated. Second, the manufacturing facility should not provide products to a number of divisions, again because the allocation process is too complicated.

This process works best in a vertically integrated company when the manufacturing facility sells most or all of its product to a marketing facility that sells only products received from one or two manufacturing facilities. The total profit received by the marketing division can be allocated back to the manufacturing facility fairly simply no matter how many different products are involved.

What is gained by this process of creating pseudo-profit centers? Some managers feel a great deal is gained, primarily because the process emphasizes the *interdependence* of the divisions involved. Ordinarily profit centers are used to emphasize the independence of the divisions involved in order to facilitate performance evaluation and motivate managers. But in a vertically integrated company, interdependence of divisions prevails rather than independence. Emphasizing this interdependence encourages the divisions to work together to achieve maximum profits. The allocation process can enhance cooperation because each division has an interest in the final profit.

This process also has several disadvantages that need to be weighed against the advantages. First, each division is motivated to push its standard costs as high as possible to increase its allocated share of the profit. When standards are too loose, actual costs tend to rise to meet the standards. Favorable variances will decline, if not disappear altogether. A company may have the illusion of cost control because of using standards but actually have high costs because of the constant upward pressure on the standard variable costs. Close attention to the problem, however, probably could keep it within acceptable bounds.

A second problem, less important than the first, is that the allocation process must be done at the corporate headquarters level. Only at that level is there sufficient cost information available to make the necessary proration. Some divisional autonomy will be lost, but in a vertically integrated company autonomy is difficult to achieve anyway. The additional loss of autonomy probably will be of little consequence. A third problem, lack of incentive to adopt cost saving techniques, is discussed fully in Chapter 3, under the contribution margin transfer pricing technique.

The allocation process shows how a profit/cost center can be converted entirely to a profit center and how vertically integrated cost centers can be made profit centers. If a company feels that it is important to maintain the profit concept, it can do so with the contribution margin transfer pricing technique. Company management, however, should remember that the profit centers created by the contribution margin transfer pricing technique are not really profit centers; they are either partly or entirely pseudo-profit centers.

When the ratio of external to internal sales is high in a profit/cost center, converting to a profit/pseudo-profit center is not harmful. Performance evaluation still can be based on profitability analysis with small loss of efficiency. When the ratio is not high in a profit/cost center that is converted to a profit/pseudo-profit center, however, care must be taken in performance evaluation. If a vertically integrated cost center is converted into a pseudo-profit center with the contribution margin technique, performance evaluation should be based on cost analysis.

To summarize, companies must use the general rule carefully in this market situation. As the ratio of external sales to internal sales declines, the reliability of a lost contribution margin based on external sales also declines. Therefore, a company would need to use some judgment in applying the general rule. If the company feels a lost contribution margin based on external sales is reliable, this LCM should be used to determine the transfer price. On the other hand, if a company feels a lost contribution margin based on external sales is not reliable, the transfer price will equal the SVC. Furthermore, for products which lack an external market price, the contribution margin transfer pricing technique can be used to maintain the profit concept.

Profit maximization will be maintained if the company accurately assesses the reliability of the lost contribution margin. When the company decides that an LCM based on external sales is reliable, it is in essence deciding that it has a known alternative to selling the products internally that will generate a contribution margin equal to the LCM. When the company decides the LCM is not reliable, it is deciding that it has an unknown or no external alternative to the internal sales. If the company's decisions are accurate, profit maximization is promoted by the general rule. Performance evaluation will be enhanced regardless of whether the company decides the LCM is reliable or unreliable, but again only if the decision is accurate. In all instances the general rule is still fairly simple.

Situation #5—Profit Center with Idle Capacity

When a profit center has idle capacity, economics dictate that the idle capacity should be utilized to manufacture a product whenever the sales price of the product exceeds the incremental costs of producing and selling it. The transfer price should, it would appear, equal the incremental production costs, but if the incremental production costs are used as the transfer price, the profit center will become a profit/cost center with the motivation problem discussed extensively in Situation #4. That is, whenever external sales production conflicts with internal sales production, a profit/cost center with a profit orientation will trade off the internal sales for external sales.

The general rule in this case will lead to using standard variable costs as the transfer price. The lost contribution margin will equal zero because there is no lost contribution. The supplying division, however, should receive an allocated share of the profit from the receiving division. The allocation can be made as described in Situation #4 or by any other method that will motivate the respective managers.

The supplying manager probably will be satisfied with any profit in excess of the standard variable costs and incremental fixed costs. Even a small profit will motivate the supplying manager because it will increase his divisional profit, which he otherwise could not do. The receiving manager may be more difficult to satisfy because he will compare his profit from the added product to his current opportunities.

It may be necessary for corporate management to monitor the situation to ensure that profitable opportunities are not lost to the company.

If for some reason the supplying division reaches production capacity and the receiving division wishes to buy amounts greater than can be produced with the previously idle capacity, the transfer price should become two-tiered. Production amounts greater than the idle capacity of the supplying division would mean that production of external sales must be sacrificed. Thus, the transfer price for production above the previously idle capacity should be the market price the supplying division could receive if it sold the product externally, or, if that is not readily available, the sum of standard variable cost plus the contribution margin lost by sacrificing production of other products sold externally. In this manner the company will maximize its profits. If the second transfer price squeezes the profit margin of the receiving division, it may be unprofitable for the receiving division to sell the additional production at the incremental selling price and difficult, if not impossible, to sell it at a higher price. If so, not manufacturing the additional production would benefit the company as a whole.

Summary of Transfer Pricing in Profit Centers

The general rule for transfer pricing is that the transfer price should equal the standard variable cost (SVC) plus the contribution margin lost (LCM) by not producing the next most profitable product, or TP = SVC + LCM. Often when profit centers are used, it is not necessary to calculate the SVC or the LCM because they sum to the market price, which is easier to determine. The market price, however, may need to be adjusted for quantifiable market imperfections, such as economies incurred by selling internally rather than externally.

When the product produced does not have a market price that can be used as the transfer price, the general rule of TP = SVC + LCM still applies. If most of the products produced by a division are sold externally, the transfer price is SVC plus LCM, where LCM is the contribution margin given up by the supplying division in order to produce products for sale internally. The determination of the LCM assumes that the productive facilities used to produce the products sold internally can be used to produce the products sold externally.

If most of the products produced in a profit center cannot be sold externally, the transfer price should equal the SVC since the LCM equals zero. This condition will create a profit/cost center. A profit/cost center manager will not be motivated to produce products that give a return equal to only the SVC, however, so a profit/cost center should be converted into a total profit center or a total cost center.

A means of converting a profit/cost division into a total profit division when the LCM on externally sold products is unreliable or cannot be determined is to allocate the profit from the ultimate sale of the product between the supplying and receiving divisions. The transfer price follows the general rule of SVC plus LCM, where LCM equals zero. The ultimate profit can be allocated by a variety of methods, one of which is to base the allocation on standard variable costs. The method used to allocate the ultimate profit, however, is separate from transfer pricing.

The allocation process also can be used to convert a cost center into a profit center when the cost center transfers most or all of its product to a marketing division. The allocation is easiest when a manufacturing facility and a marketing facility form a single profit center. Allocation of the profit realized by the marketing division makes the manufacturing facility a pseudo-profit center, which some firms may consider advantageous.

The allocation process also can be used when a profit center has short-term idle capacity. Economics dictate that if idle capacity exists, a product should be produced whenever the sales price of the product exceeds the incremental costs of production. The general rule gives a transfer price of SVC because there is no LCM. Because this rule creates a profit/cost center, the profit on the sale should be allocated between the supplying and receiving divisions so that the supplying division covers its incremental fixed costs and adds to its divisional profit.

The Use of the General Rule for Transfer Pricing with Cost Centers

Among the companies in this study, only four used cost centers at the divisional level. Three of the four said they used cost centers only because they could not use a profit center.

The companies cited two primary reasons for cost centers. First, several companies felt that the market prices of the product transferred were unreliable. One company had 150 different intermediate products that were transferred among divisions. Only 5% to 15% had reliable market prices. Another company felt it could not use the prevailing market price because its internal volume exceeded the total of all market sales by all competitors. Therefore, it faced a significantly imperfectly competitive market with an apparently nonsensical market price.

Cost centers for these companies were the only viable solution although pseudo-profit centers were a possibility.

A second reason given for using cost centers was the interdependence of vertically integrated divisions. One company felt that the interdependence of the divisions and the extensive transfers back and forth between the divisions simply made using profit centers too complicated. The company had just changed its primary transfer pricing technique from adjusted market price to standard full cost. Even when using standard full cost for transfers, it calculated the market values of the transfers from the largest division monthly and constructed a profit and loss statement. Also, transfers to subsidiaries were at the prevailing market price.

In general, profit centers were used wherever possible. Cost centers were used only where reliable market prices could not be determined for transferred products. Sometimes the market price was unreliable because the market was too thin, and at other times the company's volume would have severely affected the prevailing market price if the company sold its product externally. Occasionally the transferred product was unique, and no market price existed.

It should be noted that every company in this study used cost centers at some level in the organization. Often, however, the level at which cost centers appeared (because profit centers could not be used) was so low in the organizational structure that the volume of transfers was trivial compared to the sales volume of the divisions.

Examples of the application of the general rule to cost centers are shown in Situations #6 and #7.

Situation #6—External Prices for Products Produced Do Not Exist; or, if they do exist, are unreliable because the market is thin or more than slightly imperfectly competitive.

The application of the general rule, TP = SVC + LCM, appears simple to apply to circumstances that necessitate cost centers. Because the LCM cannot be determined, the transfer price is always the SVC, which, as was noted at the beginning of the chapter, approximates actual variable cost. But what of the fixed costs incurred by the supplying division? Can they be ignored by the receiving division?

There are two arguments for the receiving division not to ignore the fixed costs of the supplying division. The first argument is that the receiving division cannot establish proper prices without the supplying division's fixed costs. The second is that the receiving division's profitability will be distorted because it receives all the profit on products transferred-in at the SVC. Each argument will be examined in turn.[6]

If the receiving division does not take the supplying division's fixed cost into consideration when setting prices, presumably it also will ignore its own fixed costs and make pricing decisions with contribution margins. But will this practice lead to underpricing? Not necessarily, according to Charles Horngren:

> A major criticism leveled at the contribution approach is that it will result in underpricing and ultimate company disaster. Such a criticism implies that full manufacturing cost is a safer guide because it does not ignore fixed factory overhead and will therefore lead to better long-term pricing decisions.
>
> There are at least four basic weaknesses in that argument. First, full manufacturing cost also ignores some costs—the selling and administrative costs, which are often substantial. Under absorption costing, pricing decisions are often guided by unit gross profit rather than by unit net profit [NAA Research Report No. 37, p. 43]. Second, even when absorption costing is used, there is no single unit cost that may be used as a guide as long as volume is variable. Third, cost accountants and businessmen give excessive emphasis to costs as a guide to pricing. That is, they say and perhaps think that costs influence pricing decisions, but their actions show that *customer demand* and *competitor behavior* greatly overshadow cost as price-influencing factors. Fourth, an NAA survey (Report No. 37, p. 55) of 38 companies that use direct costing reported:
>
> "No instance of unprofitable pricing attributable to direct costing was reported, but, on the contrary, opinion was frequently expressed to the effect that direct costing had contributed to better pricing decisions. However, companies restrict product cost and margin data to individuals qualified to interpret such data and responsible for pricing policy decisions."[7]

Horngren's comments suggest that the SVC could be used as the transfer price without impairing pricing decisions as long as the receiving division uses the contribution margin approach to pricing. As suggested by the NAA survey, referred to by Horngren, pricing decisions might be given to a staff, perhaps on the corporate level. The resulting loss of autonomy would be negligible because companies using cost centers tend to be highly vertically integrated and, therefore, highly interdependent. Furthermore, a corporate staff, taking a company view, could ensure that the prices used generated a contribution margin in excess of the company's fixed costs. Thus, the first argument against a transfer price of SVC, that fixed costs must be transferred to the receiving division to ensure accurate pricing does not seem to be valid.

What about the second argument, that the receiving division's profitability will be distorted? This argument lacks validity also as long as the performance evaluation is based on contribution margins. When contribution margins are used to evaluate performance, all products and all divisions are on an equal basis, and cross comparisons are easy to make. If performance evaluation is not based on contribution margin analysis, however, the profitability and performance of the receiving division would be distorted by a transfer price equal to the SVC.

Therefore, it would seem that the arguments against a transfer price equal to the SVC are not very persuasive. Fixed manufacturing costs simply can remain with the division that incurred then and then be compared to standard cost. If that solution is unsatisfactory, the fixed costs can be transferred to the corporate level although many companies still may prefer that the fixed costs be transferred to the receiving division. Is it possible for these companies to use a transfer price equal to the SVC and also to transfer fixed costs to the receiving division?

One solution is to charge the supplying division's budgeted fixed costs as period costs to the divisions buying the transferred products. The budgeted fixed costs should *not* be transferred as product costs, however, since any method of allocating fixed costs to products will be arbitrary, and the supplying division's budgeted fixed costs will become the receiving division's variable cost. Treating fixed costs as variable may adversely affect pricing, but, more important, it makes it very difficult for other divisions to make optimal decisions because from their view, all transferred-in cost is variable. The inevitable result of allocating fixed costs (standard or actual) to products will be lack of profit maximization unless the company takes special care.

Therefore, in addition to the transfer price equal to the SVC, the receiving divisions will be charged periodically for the budgeted fixed costs of the supplying division. These costs should be charged to the receiving division as often as necessary, but the extent of the charge should not be based on the volume of transfers between the two divisions. The allocation of the budgeted fixed costs of the supplying division charged to each receiving division should be based on some formula that is not related to the volume of transfers between the divisions.

Once contracted for, the budgeted fixed cost charged to a division should not be changed unless unforseen circumstances cause one of the receiving divisions to severely cut back on the volume it contracted for from the supplying division. In this case, the proportion of the budgeted fixed cost to be transferred to the receiving division may be changed or even eliminated. The reduced charge should not be spread among the other receiving divisions, however, unless they wish to avail themselves of the newly released capacity of the supplying division by expanding the volume of their transfers. If not, the unallocated fixed cost should be charged to a special corporate account until the idle capacity can be utilized.

The weakness of this approach is that the allocation of the supplying division's fixed costs among the receiving divisions will be arbitrary. Thus, the ultimate profitability of a receiving division that is a profit center will be distorted and performance evaluation more difficult. Furthermore, some receiving divisions might allocate their portion of the supplying division's fixed costs among the products they receive from the supplying division. As was shown in Chapter 4, this process obscures profit analysis.

In summary, when the general rule is applied to a market situation where a product transferred by a division does not have a reliable market price, the transfer price is equal to the SVC because no LCM exists. If such products comprise a large part of the total production of the supplying division, the division will be a cost center.

A transfer price equal to the SVC will promote profit maximization and enhance performance evaluation—as well as being simple. For those companies that feel that fixed costs should be transferred to the receiving division, a process was suggested for accomplishing this transfer, but transferring fixed costs to the receiving division can create important problems.

Situation #7—Idle Capacity in a Cost Center

The circumstances of idle capacity in a cost center are similar to those discussed under Situation #5. In Situation #5 the transfer price for products produced with capacity that otherwise would be idle was the standard variable cost. In order to create a profit center with respect to the products transferred, a portion of the contribution margin of the products was transferred back to the division that produced the product.

In a cost center the transfer price also will be the standard variable cost. Because the previously idle capacity is to be treated as a cost center, no contribution margin is transferred back to the division which produced the product. Furthermore, any direct or incremental fixed costs should be transferred to the receiving division unless there is more than one receiving division. Transferring just the incremental fixed costs assumes that the previously idle capacity will be used only on a short-term basis. If the previously idle capacity is to be used on a long-term basis, the incremental fixed costs become part of the permanent fixed costs of the supplying division.

Transfer Pricing When There Are Multiple Suppliers or Multiple Receivers

When several divisions are supplying the same product, the optimal level of output for the company depends on the costs of all the suppliers. Therefore, no one supplying division is in position to determine what its level of output should be. In addition, if more than one division receives the product, coordination is needed to ensure a smooth, efficient, low-cost flow of the product between divisions. An example of multiple suppliers and multiple receivers would be mills producing ingots that are transformed into various finished products by several divisions. In determining the transfer price for multiple suppliers and multiple receivers, the general rule holds and need be adjusted only to reflect the lost contribution margin of more than one division.

When there are several supplying divisions, determination of the production level of each supplying division should be done at the *corporate* level. One firm studied established a planning committee made up of executives of the supplying and receiving divisions. This committee met monthly to determine the production levels and internal transfers of each supplying division. Since each supplying division was a profit center with external sales, the planning committee assessed the profit opportunities of the various supplying and receiving divisions and allocated production on the basis of maximum company profit.

Another company which used cost centers established a department whose responsibilities included ensuring the efficient flow of internal products. The supplying divisions competed against each other on the basis of actual cost compared to standard cost. Full standard costs were used to transfer all products out of the supplying divisions. The full standard costs of all the supplying divisions were averaged, and the average was used to transfer the product to the receiving divisions.

The transfer pricing technique applicable to multiple suppliers and multiple receivers is still determined using the general rule. What is different is that profit maximization, the second criterion, cannot be achieved without central coordination of the activities of the divisions involved. Profit centers, seeking to maximize their own profits, may make decisions that benefit their division but not the company. Cost centers, seeking to compete on a basis of cost minimization, may not be candid about cost savings innovations.

EXHIBIT 5-11

The Company Contribution Margin

Assume that Division A can sell to Division B or it can sell externally. If Division A sells externally, the external purchaser also will buy some additional products from Division C. The figures involved are shown below.

	Division A	Division B	Division C
MP	$ 13	$ 18	$ 6
VC	(7)	(4)	(4)
VC-A	—	(7)	—
CM/PU	$ 6	$ 7	$ 2
Units	× 100	× 100	× 100
CM	$600	$700	$200

If Division A sells externally, it will earn a contribution margin of $600, while Division C will earn $200, giving a company contribution margin of $800. If Division A sells to Division B, both Division B and the company will earn a contribution margin of $700. Therefore, the profit maximizing action is for Division A to sell externally. The transfer price should be the sum of the standard variable cost of Division A, $7, and the lost contribution margin of Divisions A and C, ($6 + $2 = $8), for a total of $15. A transfer price of $15 gives Division B a contribution margin per unit of ($1), so it will not buy from Division A. Thus, company profits are maximized.

A Company-Wide Perspective of the General Rule

Early in this chapter the general rule was given: The transfer price should equal the standard variable cost (SVC) plus the contribution margin given up *by the company,* referred to as the lost contribution margin (LCM), when a segment sells internally. Throughout the chapter it was assumed that the lost contribution margin of the supplying division equaled the lost contribution margin of the company. Most of the time this will be true, but occasionally it will not. An example of applying the general rule when the lost contribution margin of the division is not equal to that of the firm is shown in Exhibit 5-11.

As the example shows, the transfer price is the sum of standard variable cost of the product sold internally by Division A and the contribution margin per unit lost by Divisions A and C. If Division C can sell its product to someone other than the customer of Division A at the same price, Division C can be ignored and the transfer price set at $13 ($7 + $6 = $13). If Division C loses part of its contribution margin when selling to someone other than the customer of Division A, the transfer price should include the amount of contribution margin lost. Whatever the situation, the general rule will still apply.

Summary

In this chapter the proposed general rule of transfer pricing was presented: The transfer price (TP) should equal the standard variable cost (SVC) plus the lost contribution margin (LCM) of the company, or TP = SVC + LCM. The general rule fits all situations and can be used for determining the appropriate transfer price in profit centers, pseudo-profit centers, and cost centers. A summary of the application of the general rule to the situations discussed in this chapter is shown under "Highlights of Results" in Chapter 1. A brief summary is shown next.

Environmental Situation	General Rule	Responsibility Center
1. Perfectly competitive markets	TP = SVC + LCM = prevailing market price	Profit center
2. Imperfectly competitive markets		
A. Slightly imperfectly competitive	TP = SVC + LCM = adjusted market price	Profit center

Environmental Situation	General Rule	Responsibility Center
B. Moderately imperfectly competitive	TP = SVC because LCM is 0	Cost center
C. Significantly imperfectly competitive	TP = SVC because LCM is 0	Cost center
3. Most products sold externally in a perfectly competitive or slightly imperfectly competitive market. Products sold internally do not have a market price. Production capacity used to produce internally sold products *can* be used to produce externally sold products.	TP = SVC + LCM = phantom market price	Profit center
4. A. Most or all products sold internally, and transferred products do not have a reliable market price; or	TP = SVC because LCM is 0	Cost center should be used. A pseudo-profit center can be created, however, using the contribution margin transfer pricing technique.
B. Most products are sold externally, but production capacity used to produce internally sold products *cannot* be used to produce externally sold products.	TP = SVC because LCM is 0	Pseudo-profit center for products transferred. The profit concept can be maintained by the contribution margin transfer pricing technique.
5. Profit center with idle capacity	TP = SVC because LCM is 0	Pseudo-profit center for products produced using the otherwise idle capacity. The contribution margin technique can be used.
6. External prices for products produced do not exist.	TP = SVC because LCM is 0	Cost center
7. Idle capacity in a cost center	TP = SVC because LCM is 0	Cost center

The core of the general rule is determining the LCM. When an accurate LCM can be determined, the transfer price will represent the best alternative available to the supplying division. As long as Division A had an alternative to selling its product to Division B, an LCM can be calculated. Otherwise the transfer price is equal to the SVC because the LCM will equal zero.

On occasion a transfer price equal to the SVC will create a profit/cost center. If the products transferred at the SVC represent a small proportion of the total production of the supplying division, the contribution margin transfer pricing technique can be used to restore the supplying division to a total profit center. The contribution margin technique, however, is not without problems and should be used with caution. Creating a pseudo-profit center from a responsibility center that produces products mostly or entirely without external market prices is not recommended.

In some ways the general rule represents very little departure from current transfer pricing practices because it often leads to using a well-known transfer pricing technique. The principal value of the general rule is that when applied it will lead the company to a technique that (1) promotes profit maximization in almost all instances, (2) enhances performance evaluation, and (3) is understood easily. The general rule shows that a number of currently used transfer pricing techniques are based on a common factor, SVC + LCM, but that market characteristics and management philosophy have made related transfer pricing techniques appear very different.

In one way the general rule represents a substantial departure from current practice because the general rule treats all fixed costs as period costs. The common practice among the businesses in this study was to treat fixed costs as product costs and allocate these costs directly to the product, thereby affecting the transfer price. Business will make fewer errors by utilizing contribution margins in decision making rather than treating fixed costs as if they were variable.

Notes

1. The symbols used in this exhibit and others are as follows: MP = market price; SVC = standard variable cost; TP = transfer price, CM/PU = contribution margin per unit; CM = contribution margin.
2. In this exhibit and others it is assumed that Division B sells a number of products and that discontinuing purchases from Division A does not imply that Division B will go out of business or that it must purchase the product

from a competitor of Division A. The assumption is made, however, only to facilitate the exhibits. If Division A must sell to Division B or Division B must buy from Division A or both, the general rule still applies.

3. Of course, this situation does not occur only when Division B has a negative contribution. A more likely situation would be that Division B has a positive contribution margin if it buys the product from Division A, but the contribution margin is lower than Division B can attain from other opportunities. Thus, even with a positive contribution margin, Division B may decide not to buy from Division A, which can lead to lower company profits.
4. In a perfectly competitive market the demand curve is horizontal, while in a slightly imperfectly competitive market the demand curve is very nearly horizontal.
5. Hirschleifer shows that the optimal level, which he refers to as the equilibrium level, is at the point where the sum of the marginal costs of Divisions A and B intersect the marginal revenue. Hirschleifer's analysis also results in a two-tiered transfer price. See Jack Hirschleifer, "On the Economics of Transfer Pricing," *Journal of Business,* (July 1956), pp. 172-184.
6. The problems associated with inventory valuation are separate from those of pricing and profitability analysis. The latter are economic decisions, while the former is a financial accounting decision complicated by assumed flows of product, e.g., FIFO and LIFO, from raw materials inventory to cost of goods sold. It does not make any difference how fixed costs are allocated to products for inventory valuation as long as the resulting cost is not used as a transfer price nor for pricing decisions and profitability analysis.
7. Charles Horngren, *Cost Accounting: A Managerial Emphasis,* Prentice-Hall, Inc., Englewood Cliffs, N.J., 1977, p. 342.

Chapter 6

International Transfer Pricing and Tax Objectives

The advent of U.S.-based multinational corporations and their continued growth have added another, more complicated dimension to transfer pricing. The complications arise because international transfer pricing must meet not only the objectives of the management control process, but also a wide variety of other objectives. These other objectives are sometimes so important that the objectives of goal congruence (profit maximization) and performance evaluation are considered secondary or unachievable. Thus, it is important that the type of objectives involved in international transfer pricing and their effect on transfer prices be understood thoroughly.

This chapter is divided into two closely related sections. The first section is a discussion of additional objectives a company might consider when establishing prices for transfers across national boundaries. The second section elaborates on one of these objectives, tax minimization, with a discussion of Section 482 of the Internal Revenue Code and its implications for international transfer pricing.

International Transfer Pricing Objectives

In establishing international transfer prices, a firm must try to satisfy a number of objectives not relevant to domestic transfer pricing. For example, the firm wants to minimize taxes and at the same time win approval from the government of the host country. Yet the basic objectives of profit maximization and performance evaluation also are important. Often it is not possible to satisfy all these objectives simultaneously, so a company must decide which objectives are the most important. As a result, a particular transfer price, rather than evolving from a transfer pricing technique, may be established arbitrarily to fulfill an objective involving international considerations. The discussion that follows examines some of these objectives.[1]

Income Tax Minimization

By far the most persuasive objective in international transfer pricing is tax minimization. The economic advantages are obvious and immediate if a transfer price shifts profit from a country with a high tax rate to a country with a low tax rate. For example, if a product is being manufactured in a country with a favorable tax structure, a high transfer price will result in more of the profit from the sale of the product being taxed at the favorable rate. An example of using transfer pricing to minimize income taxes is shown in Exhibit 6-1.

As the example in Exhibit 6-1 has shown, tax minimization via transfer pricing is a simple process. When a firm minimizes taxes by shifting profit between countries, however, other objectives of transfer pricing, such as performance evaluation and profit maximization, may become harder, if not impossible, to attain.

On the surface it would appear that tax minimization would meet the objective of profit maximization, but whether it does or not depends upon the specific circumstances. It is unlikely, however, that a transfer price which minimizes taxes also will guide a company toward profit-maximizing decisions such as whether to sell a product internally or externally or whether to invest in additional productive facilities. Furthermore, a program of tax minimization may result in different transfer prices for the same product transferred to different countries, so foreign affiliates in different countries will have different transfer prices with which to make other profit maximizing decisions.

The other objective, performance evaluation, is even more difficult to attain when the objective of tax minimization is pursued. The profit in one country will be greater than the profit in another country, not because of better management but because of the transfer price. One way around this problem is to establish a separate reporting system for control purposes so performance evaluation is based on more realistic reports.

The tax rate is not the only factor to consider in tax minimization because countries have different requirements for calculating taxable income. Even though Country A has a tax rate of 20% on all taxable income and Country B has a 40% rate, total taxes may be lower in

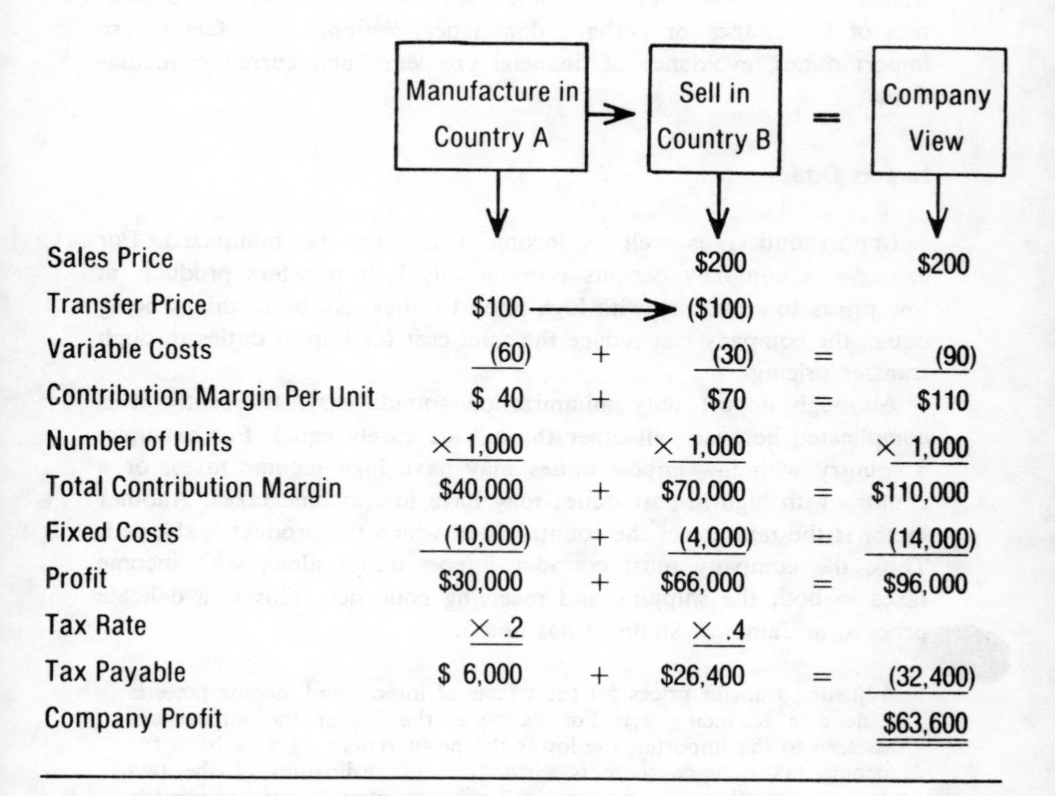

EXHIBIT 6-1

Tax Minimization

	Manufacture in Country A		Sell in Country B		Company View
Sales Price			$200		$200
Transfer Price	$100	→	($100)		
Variable Costs	(60)	+	(30)	=	(90)
Contribution Margin Per Unit	$ 40	+	$70	=	$110
Number of Units	× 1,000		× 1,000		× 1,000
Total Contribution Margin	$40,000	+	$70,000	=	$110,000
Fixed Costs	(10,000)	+	(4,000)	=	(14,000)
Profit	$30,000	+	$66,000	=	$96,000
Tax Rate	× .2		× .4		
Tax Payable	$ 6,000	+	$26,400	=	(32,400)
Company Profit					$63,600

In the example above, the transfer price of $100 per unit results in $30,000 of the ultimate profit of $96,000 remaining in the country with the 20% tax rate. Clearly, it is to the economic benefit of the company to raise the transfer price as high as the government in Country B will allow. In so doing, more of the profit is shifted into Country A and taxed at a lower rate.

For example, if the government of Country B will allow a transfer price of $150 per unit, $50,000 of the $70,000 contribution margin in Country B will be shifted back to Country A, giving Country A a total contribution margin of $90,000 with tax of $16,000. The tax in Country B will decline from $26,400 to $6,400. Thus, a transfer price of $150 per unit gives the same before-tax profit of $96,000 but increases the after-tax profit from $63,600 to $73,600 because of the $10,000 reduction in total tax.

Country B if, for example, Country A severely restricts deductions for depreciation while Country B does not.

Although income taxation is the most persuasive objective to influence transfer prices, other objectives will from time to time assume a position of importance or perhaps dominance. Among these factors are import duties, avoidance of financial problems, and currency fluctuations.

Import Duties

Import duties, as well as income taxes, can be minimized. For example, a company benefits economically if it transfers products at low prices to a country with high import duties. All other things being equal, the company can reduce the total cost for import duties through transfer pricing.

Although import duty minimization sounds easy, frequently it is complicated because "all other things" are rarely equal. For example, a country with low import duties may have high income taxes, or a country with high import duties may have low income taxes. Another factor is the tax rate of the country from which the product is shipped. Thus, the company must consider import duties along with income taxes in both the shipping and receiving countries. This is a delicate process, as James S. Shulman has noted:

> Adjusting transfer prices for the effects of import and income taxes is a delicate balancing act. For example, the higher the import tax assessed to the importer, the lower the profit remaining as a basis for income taxes. Since there is virtually no coordination of the two revenue-collecting departments in [most countries], the income-tax collecting branch may be unduly exercised. An added difficulty results from the attempt of the parent to balance the extra cost of duty resulting from a high import price paid by its affiliate against the lower income taxes that the affiliate will be charged with, as well as the potentially higher income taxes that the exporting affiliate may be required to remit.[2]

Balancing import duties and income taxes is more complicated than simply minimizing taxes. In order to minimize import duties and income taxes in Belgium, the receiving country, and income taxes in two shipping countries, one company in this study invoiced identical goods into Belgium at different prices. The different prices drew the attention of customs officials and income-tax authorities. The result was a comprehensive review of pricing practices used by the company in Belgium, which led to required changes in pricing practices and higher total income taxes. In addition, the investigation had a ripple effect. Other countries learned of the investigation, and several started comprehensive reviews of the company's pricing practices in their countries. In addition to all-around higher income taxes, the company suffered a great deal of bad publicity.

Minimization of income taxes and import duties is an important goal. Recently, however, taxing authorities in many countries have begun to pay closer attention to attempts by companies to transfer profit to countries with lower taxes. As one unfortunate company discovered, overzealous efforts to minimize import duties and taxes may result in short-run gains but long-run losses.

Avoiding Financial Problems

Transfer pricing often can be used to circumvent economic restrictions placed on multinational companies by host countries. For example, Israel places severe restrictions on the amount of profit that can leave the country. A way around this is to charge high prices for imports. Of course, a country that imposes such a restriction probably will watch import and export prices closely.

A second economic restriction by some countries is disallowing certain expenses against taxable income. For example, some general administrative expenses or research and development expenses may be disallowed if they are performed elsewhere. Another example is royalty fees charged by management against subsidiary income. To the extent these are disallowed by the host country, the amounts can be recaptured by increasing the price of goods shipped into the country.

Transfer pricing also can be used to improve the financial condition of an affiliate, thereby presenting a favorable profit picture to satisfy earnings criteria by foreign lenders. In this manner the parent company can avoid committing capital to a foreign affiliate, even though the affiliate may be required to secure the loan. Furthermore, besides improving the affiliate's financial picture, low transfer prices provide the affiliate a competitive edge that can be very useful during the startup period of a new venture.

Currency Fluctuations

During periods of currency instability, the performance reports of foreign affiliates can be affected dramatically by exchange rate fluctuations. Many United States-based multinational companies find it convenient to evaluate the performance of foreign affiliates with reports stated in U.S. dollars. If currency exchange rates fluctuate during the performance period, however, it may be difficult to evaluate the performance of the affiliate. At the same time, management of the affiliate often finds it more convenient to evaluate its performance with reports stated in local currency rather than U.S. dollars.

This performance evaluation problem is compounded by transfer pricing unless the transfer price changes with changes in currency values. The difficulties that arise when the transfer prices are not adjusted for currency exchange fluctuations and a proposed solution have been illustrated by Duane Malmstrom and are shown in Exhibits 6-2 and 6-3 respectively.[3]

As a simple solution to the difficulties illustrated in Exhibit 6-2, Malmstrom proposes an indexing formula. The formula, which he refers to as dollar indexing, is shown below:

$$NTP = OTP \times \frac{CER}{PER}$$

Where

NTP = New transfer price
OTP = Old transfer price
CER = Current exchange rate
PER = Planned exchange rate

This formula is applied in Exhibit 6-3.

Malmstrom's dollar indexing formula is both simple and effective. The formula is similar to formulae used for price-level adjustments in inflation accounting. Furthermore, just as inflation accounting can isolate price-level gains and losses, Malmstrom's dollar indexing formula can isolate operational results and exchange fluctuation results. It also should be noted that the indexing formula shifts the burden of foreign currency fluctuation to Subsidiary A who is in the best position to make decisions that are affected by the fluctuations.

Summary of International Objectives

A number of international objectives have been discussed — income

EXHIBIT 6-2

Transfer Prices not Adjusted for Currency Exchange Fluctuations

Under fixed United States dollar transfer pricing, performance measurement is distorted whenever the actual exchange rates for the producing or purchasing country deviate from the planned exchange rate. For example, suppose Subsidiary A (a manufacturing location) plans to produce and sell 1,000 devices to its affiliated subsidiaries at $10 per unit, the approved transfer price. Suppose also that Subsidiary A's total local currency cost to produce these devices is LCA 18,000 and that the planned exchange rate is $1.00 = LCA2. Thus, the planned P&L's for Subsidiary A, measured in United States dollars and in local currency, will be:

Subsidiary A—Plan

	United States dollars	Exchange rate	Local currency
Sales (inter-company)	$10,000	$1.00 = LCA2	LCA 20,000
Costs	9,000	LCA1 = $.50	18,000
Profit	$ 1,000		LCA 2,000
Percent of sales	10		10

Now suppose that the year actually progresses exactly as planned, except that the United States dollar devalues so that $1.00 = LCA1. Thus, the actual P&L results for Subsidiary A measured in United States dollars and in local currency will be:

Subsidiary A—Results

	United States dollars	Exchange rate	Local currency
Sales (inter-company)	$10,000	$1.00 = LCA1	LCA 10,000
Costs	18,000	LCA1 = $1.00	18,000
Profit	$(8,000)		LCA (8,000)
Percent of sales	(80)		(80)

As you can see, even though Subsidiary A actually achieved planned device volume and controlled its local currency manufacturing costs precisely as planned, its profit performance was completely obliterated by the exchange rate change. This "distortion" occurred in both the United States dollar P&L and in the local currency P&L.

EXHIBIT 6-3
Transfer Prices Adjusted for Currency Exchange Fluctuation

Consider what would happen if all suppositions were the same as in [Exhibit 6-2], except that dollar indexing was in effect. Since Subsidiary A's planned exchange rate was LCA1 = $.50, but the actual exchange rate was LCA1 = $1.00, its dollar transfer prices would be increased through the use of the formula:

$$NTP = OTP \times \frac{CER}{PER}$$

$$= \$10 \times \frac{\$1.00}{\$\ .50}$$

$$= \$20.00 \text{ per device}$$

Assuming that actual volumes were achieved, at planned local currency costs, Subsidiary A's actual P&L results would be:

Subsidiary A—Results

	United States dollars	Exchange rate	Local currency
Sales (inter-company)	$20,000	$1.00 = LCA1	LCA 20,000
Çosts	18,000	LCA1 = $1.00	18,000
Profit	$ 2,000		LCA 2,000
Percent of sales	10		10

As you can see, Subsidiary A actually achieves its planned profit rate, measured in dollars and local currency. Thus, under dollar indexing, factory performance is not distorted due to exchange rate fluctuations.

tax minimization, import duty minimization, adjusting for currency fluctuations, avoiding economic restrictions, and presenting a favorable financial picture of a foreign affiliate in order to enhance borrowing opportunities or provide a temporary competitive edge. These objectives are not always compatible with the objectives of the management control process, goal congruence (profit maximization) and performance evaluation, so a firm sometimes must maintain one set of books for foreign authorities and another set for parent company performance evaluation purposes.

Sometimes the practice of maintaining two sets of books causes problems. The books used for foreign authorities are likely to be the best known set both inside and outside the company. Managers of foreign affiliates that are profitable by virtue of favorable transfer prices may assume an unjustified aura of superiority over managers of affiliates that are subject to less favorable transfer prices. The parent company management also may overlook, at least temporarily, the source of a profit of a foreign affiliate that enjoys favorable transfer prices. If these situations occur, and they are likely to at least to a small degree, they can cause hard feelings between foreign affiliates or between the parent and foreign affiliates.

In addition, a company must be at least prudent and probably cautious in establishing and changing transfer prices. Authorities in other countries are becoming increasingly sophisticated, and even among third world countries, blatent efforts to shift profit to the obvious detriment of a country will be detected quickly and dealt with swiftly. A considerable amount of goodwill may be lost. On the other hand, a company that consistently pursues policies designed to satisfy to the greatest extent possible the taxing authorities of all host countries, even at some economic sacrifice, can build up goodwill. One company in this study, in order to be as even-handed as possible, established all transfer prices so that the profit on transferred products was split 50-50 between the sending country and the receiving country. This policy ended the many difficulties the company had with taxing authorities, particularly in Europe.

As noted earlier, in spite of the varied international objectives that can be accomplished by transfer pricing, income tax and import duty minimization seem to dominate international transfer pricing decisions.

Section 482 of the Internal Revenue Code and Transfer Pricing

As noted previously, tax minimization is one of the most persuasive objectives in international transfer pricing because of the immediate economic benefits involved. Tax minimization, however, must be pursued cautiously. Host country governments understandably are very sensitive to transfer prices, so a thorough understanding of tax regulations of host countries is necessary to avoid difficulties.

In the United States, transfer pricing is covered by Section 482 of that in any case of two or more companies owned or controlled by the same interest, the Internal Revenue Service (IRS) may distribute, apportion or allocate gross income or deductions between or among the businesses if it determines that it is necessary to do so in order to prevent evasion of taxes or reflect clearly the income of the businesses involved. Section 482 sets forth allocation rules for specific items:

(1) Imputed interest on intercompany loans and advances;
(2) Services performed by one member for another;
(3) Use of tangible property;
(4) Pricing of intercompany sales of tangible property;
(5) Transfers of intangible property.

Of these five specific items, this study is concerned with only (4), which covers transfer pricing of tangible property.

How does Section 482 affect transfer pricing of tangible property? In a typical case, a United States parent company sells goods to its foreign affiliate for resale. If the IRS finds that the price to the affiliate was below an arm's-length price, it adjusts the taxable income of the parent to reflect the higher arm's-length price. The result is an increase in the parent's U.S. tax liability. The foreign affiliate, however, will have taken the lower price into account in computing its cost of goods sold and its foreign tax. Therefore, unless the foreign government allows the affiliate to correspondingly adjust its foreign taxes, double taxation will occur. While the foreign tax credit provisions of the U.S. Internal Revenue Code can offset the double taxation to some extent, only in rare cases will it do this completely.

The threat of double taxation is no longer as great as it once was, however, because the United States government has entered into a number of tax treaties with foreign governments. These treaties contain a provision, generally referred to as the Related Persons Article, that mitigates the problem of double taxation. This provision, which is similar to Section 482 of the U.S. IRC, expresses mutual recognition of the principle of allocation of income and deductions among related persons when their dealings have not been at arm's-length; the provision also recognizes the right of the countries to continue to propose and make allocations which will reflect arm's-length dealings pursuant to their domestic laws.

The important feature of pursuing tax minimization is to ensure that transfer prices reflect arm's-length transactions as much as possible. In determining the arm's-length price for the sale of tangible property between a U.S. parent and foreign affiliate, Section 482 and related regulations allow three pricing methods. These methods are the comparable uncontrolled price method, resale price method, and cost-plus method. Each of these methods will be examined in detail, followed by methods that might be allowed by the IRS.

Comparable Uncontrolled Price Method

Reg. 1.482-2(3)(1)(i) defines an arm's-length price as the price an unrelated party would have paid under the same set of circumstances for the property involved in the controlled sale. The IRS views the comparable uncontrolled price method as the most reliable indication of an arm's-length price because it reflects (1) the price of sales made by a controlled group to an unrelated party, (2) the price of sales made by an unrelated party to a controlled group, or (3) the price of sales between parties that are not members of the same controlled group and, therefore, are unrelated to each other.[4] Thus, the comparable uncontrolled price method is actually the prevailing market price transfer pricing technique.

As was noted in Chapter 3, however, the prevailing market price rarely can be used because perfectly competitive markets are necessary. Recognizing this constraint, the IRS allows the use of the adjusted market price transfer price when the market is slightly imperfectly competitive. The IRC reads:

> Uncontrolled sales are considered comparable to controlled sales if the physical property and circumstances involved in the uncontrolled sales are identical to the physical property and circumstances involved in the controlled sales, or if such properties and circumstances are so nearly identical that any differences either have no effect on price, or such differences can be reflected by a reasonable number of adjustments to the price of uncontrolled sales.[5]

Some adjustments that are allowed are for differences in the quality of the product, terms of sale, intangible property associated with the sale, time of sale, terms of delivery, and the level of the market (i.e., wholesale, retail) and the geographic market in which the sale takes place. These adjustments are a reflection of a slightly imperfectly competitive market. Thus, Section 482 allows the prevailing market price to be adjusted for identifiable and quantifiable market imperfections when small dollar amounts are involved.[6] In other words, Section 482 sanctions use of the adjusted market price, which is derived from the general rule for transfer pricing proposed by this study.

On the other hand, Section 482 places a rather severe restriction on the determination of the adjusted market price because it allows only as many adjustments as are used with sales requiring the fewest and simplest adjustments. See the following example.

> Thus, for example, if a taxpayer makes comparable uncontrolled sales of a particular product which differ from the controlled sale only with respect to the terms of delivery, and makes other comparable uncontrolled sales of the product which differ from the controlled sale with respect to both terms of delivery and terms of payment, the comparable uncontrolled sales differing only with respect to terms of delivery should be selected as the comparable uncontrolled sale.[7]

There is no evidence that Section 482 allows adjustments for economies from selling internally, probably because it is difficult to verify the accuracy of the amounts. The principal internal economy is selling expenses, which would be difficult to determine precisely. A fairly accurate estimate could be made, however, that would not be too different in nature from some of the estimates already allowed by the IRC.

One effect of not allowing adjustments for internal economies is that additional tax revenues accrue to the United States. Not adjusting the transfer price downward for internal economies results in higher profit and higher U.S. taxes.

In addition, Section 482 allows transfers at less than the uncontrolled price for a short period if the primary purpose is to establish or maintain a market for the product transferred. For example, a company might want to make transfers at less than the comparable uncontrolled price in order to meet competition or introduce a new product.[8]

In summary, Section 482 specifies that when establishing transfer prices, a company first must attempt to apply the comparable uncontrolled price method. This method is similar to the prevailing market price transfer pricing technique discussed in Chapter 3, but the Section 482 implicitly recognizes that the perfectly competitive markets necessary to support the use of the prevailing market price rarely occur. Therefore, it allows the use of the adjusted market price, which is used with slightly imperfectly competitive markets, but restricts the number of adjustments that can be made to the prevailing market price. If a comparable uncontrolled price cannot be found, the Section specifies that the next method the company must attempt to apply is the resale price method.

Resale Price Method

The resale price method is explained best by an example from Section 482:

> Thus, where one member of a group of controlled entities sells property to another member which resells the property in uncontrolled sales, if the applicable resale price of the property involved in the controlled sale is $100 and the appropriate markup percentage for resales by the buyer is 20%, the arm's length price of the controlled sale is $80 ($100 minus 20% × $100).[9]

The arm's-length price is equal to the sales price received for the property by the reseller less an appropriate markup. Although this seems fairly simple, there are at least two problems that must be addressed before the method can be used. The first problem involves the circumstances under which this method must be used. The section lists four circumstances that must exist:

(1) There are no comparable uncontrolled sales.

(2) An applicable resale price . . . is available with respect to resales made within a reasonable time before or after the time of the controlled sale.

(3) The buyer (reseller) has not added more than an insubstantial amount to the value of the property by physically altering the product for resale. For this purpose packaging, repacking, labeling or minor assembly of property does not constitute physical alteration.

(4) The buyer (reseller) has not added more than an insubstantial amount to the value of the property by the use of intangible property.[10]

Circumstances (3) and (4) would severely curtail the use of this method, but the section allows the resale price method to be used even though circumstances (3) and (4) do not exist, if the method is more feasible and is likely to result in a more accurate determination of an arm's-length price than would the use of the cost-plus method. This exception is allowed because there may be conditions under which a buyer (reseller) might add more than an insubstantial amount to the value of the property, but the amount may be determined with reasonable precision. Thus, the resale price method might be preferable to the cost-plus method if the appropriate gross profit percentage under the cost-plus method is more difficult to determine than the appropriate markup percentage under the resale price method.

The second problem involves determining the appropriate markup percentage, which is defined as follows:

> The appropriate markup percentage is equal to the percentage of gross profit (expressed as a percentage of sales) earned by the buyer (reseller) or another party on the resale of property which is both purchased and resold in an uncontrolled transaction, which resale is most similar to the applicable resale of property involved in the controlled sale.[11]

The resale price method is essentially a work-back method of establishing an arm's-length price. The final sales price, referred to in the IRC as the applicable resale price, is determined first. Working backward from the final sales price involves subtracting an appropriate markup percentage, which is the percentage of gross profit (expressed as a percentage of sales) earned by the buyer (reseller) or others on the resale of similar property bought from and resold to unrelated parties under similar circumstances. This might be characterized as an arm's-length markup.

The markup percentages should be derived from uncontrolled purchases and sales of the buyer (reseller) in the controlled sale because of the probability that the buyer (reseller) will sell the same or similar items under uncontrolled circumstances. If resale by the buyer (reseller) is not a good indication of the markup percentage, the markup percentage of a competitor engaged in a similar business may be used although this figure rarely would be available. In the absence of more precise information, industry averages might be used.

Although the resale price method is not related directly to any of the transfer pricing techniques discussed in Chapters 3 and 4 or the general rule in Chapter 5, it is somewhat similar to the contribution margin transfer pricing technique. The resale price method is a means of allocating the profit on products purchased internally and resold by the buyer, using the markup percentage as the allocation method. For example, assume that a product produced by a company for $60 is sold for $100. If the appropriate markup percentage is 15%, the buyer (reseller) is allocated $15 of the profit with the remainder going to the manufacturing division.

In summary, Section 482 requires the use of the resale price method if the comparable uncontrolled price method cannot be used and if the resale price method is more appropriate than the cost-plus method. The resale price method is based on the belief that after a buyer (reseller) subtracts the appropriate markup percentage from the resale price, the resulting balance should be an approximation of an arm's-length transaction. The method can be used only if the appropriate markup percentage can be determined and if an accurately determinable or insubstantial amount is added to the value of the property by the buyer (reseller). If neither the comparable uncontrolled price method nor the resale price method is appropriate, the cost-plus method should be used.

Cost-Plus Method

The cost-plus method, which is almost identical to the cost-plus transfer pricing technique, is a work-forward method of constructing an arm's-length price. The cost-plus method is used when the buyer (reseller) adds *substantial* value to property before resale. For example, the cost-plus method will be used when the seller is merely engaged in purchasing property for resale and delivery to a buyer who further processes the property in a manufacturing activity or incorporates it into another product in a major assembly operation.

Essentially, the cost-plus method is an alternative to the resale price method. Generally it is more suitable than the resale price method if the cost and profit factors associated with the seller's functions are easier to evaluate than the cost and profit factors associated with the buyer's functions. In general, the approach to the cost-plus method is fairly liberal, as can be seen by the following statement:

> The cost of producing the property involved in the controlled sale and the costs which enter into the computation of the appropriate gross profit percentage [the plus] shall be computed in a consistent manner in accordance with sound accounting practices for allocating or apportioning costs, which neither favors nor burdens controlled sales in comparison with uncontrolled sales.[12]

The passage implies that the calculation of cost for property in a controlled sale should be the same as for property in an uncontrolled sale. Furthermore, a company is not constrained to one method of determining cost, such as full actual cost. Although the regulations do not define the phase "cost of producing," it is probably safe to assume that cost of producing includes all costs associated with manufacturing and distributing the product, including the cost of acquiring property used in production.

The means of finding the appropriate gross profit percentage are similar to finding the appropriate markup percentage under the resale price method. If possible, the gross profit percentage should be based on uncontrolled sales of the same or similar products made by the producer of the product. If this method cannot be used, the gross profit percentage of a competitor can be used, or, as a final resort, industry figures can be used.

In the case of *Eli Lilly and Co. v. U.S.*,[13] the IRS used the gross profit percentage on domestic sales, which were deemed to be arm's-length sales, as the appropriate gross profit percentage for international sales. Ultimately, however, the IRS reduced the proposed markup on cost of goods sold by 50% while leaving the gross profit percentage for other expenses the same. This process was accepted by the court, even though it was somewhat arbitrary, because it was not considered to have reached unreasonable results. In *Frank v. International Canadian Corp.*,[14] the Commissioner argued that the standard to be applied was whether the price arrived at was an arm's-length price and not whether the price was a reasonable one.

These two cases illustrate the arbitrary nature of the cost-plus method. The appropriate gross profit percentage is often a subjective figure even under the best of circumstances, but subsequent manipulations of this figure only serve to move the cost-plus price further away from reality. The result is often simply arbitration between the taxpayer and the IRS over the amount of the plus.

When these three methods of establishing transfer prices — the comparable uncontrolled price method, the resale price method, and the cost-plus method — were first specified, many taxpayers complained that none of the three methods was suitable for their companies. As a result the IRS allowed a fourth alternative as described by the following passage from the IRC:

> Where the standards for applying one of the three methods of pricing . . . are met, such method must, for the purposes of this paragraph, be utilized unless the taxpayer can establish that, considering all the facts and circumstances, some method of pricing other than those described . . . is clearly more appropriate. Where none of the three methods of pricing described . . . can reasonably be applied under the facts and circumstances as they exist in a particular case, some appropriate method of pricing other than those described. . . , or variations on such methods, can be used.[15]

Some methods that might be allowed by the IRS are described briefly in the next section.

Other Methods

How far the IRS is willing to go in allowing other methods is difficult to determine, but it is likely that the method proposed by the taxpayer will be analyzed to determine whether it resulted in an arm's-length transfer price. Some methods that might be accepted by the IRS are described briefly.[16]

1. *Pricing Component Parts*—The arm's-length price of a manufactured product could be estimated by adding the prices charged by unrelated parties for the various components of the completed product.
2. *Supply Substitute Material Method*—Rather than using the final selling price or gross profit percentages of the products involved in the controlled sale, the price or gross profit percentages of products in the same general class are used if they are the result of uncontrolled sales and the products in these uncontrolled sales are substituted for the products in the uncontrolled sale without a significant change in the taxpayer's resources.
3. *Appraisal Method*—The arm's-length price is the price at which an unrelated party would agree to buy the products in an untrolled sale.
4. *Proportionate Profits Method*—This method is identical to the contribution margin transfer pricing technique described in Chapter 3. The total profit on the product is allocated between the segments, using full cost as the allocation basis.
5. *Rate of Return on Investment Methods*—The profit factor in the markup percentage or gross margin percentage is based on receiving a certain rate of return on invested assets. This method is a variation of the resale price and cost-plus methods.

Without judging any of these techniques, one can see that they range from simple variations of one of the three specified techniques to wholesale departures from any known technique. Actually, the techniques mentioned above probably have little applicability to the taxpayer. The IRS has for the most part preferred that the taxpayer use one of the three specified methods.

An important question, then, is the extent to which the specified methods proposed by the IRS are compatible with the general rule for transfer prices proposed in this study.

The IRS Methods and the General Rule

The fundamental differences between the objectives of the tax authorities and the objectives of corporate transfer pricing cause rather severe discrepancies between the transfer pricing methods allowed by the IRS and the general rule. For example, recall that the objectives of transfer pricing in organizations are to promote goal congruence (profit maximization) and to enhance performance evaluation. The IRS, on the other hand, has the objective of determining a fair means of allocating the total profit of a sale between the United States and other countries. As long as the means are deemed fair and acceptable to the parties involved, it makes little difference to the IRS whether profit maximization is promoted or performance evaluation is enhanced.

A further problem is that in order for the IRS to assess taxes, a company must determine a profit. Thus, when the general rule would lead to using cost centers, a profit would have to be added, thereby resulting in a pseudo-profit center. With cost centers, the cost-plus method probably would be used to determine transfer prices for tax purposes, but such prices would not necessarily promote profit maximization or enhance performance evaluation.

In spite of the differences between the objectives of the IRS and the objectives of transfer pricing in corporations, there are occasions where the general rule and the comparable uncontrolled price method will result in identical or nearly identical transfer prices. These occasions occur when there is a prevailing market price in a perfectly competitive market or one that can be revised to an adjusted market price when the market is slightly imperfectly competitive. Although Section 482 does not specifically allow for adjustments of economies from selling internally, a strong argument for its use as part of the comparable uncontrolled price probably could be made. If so, the general rule and comparable uncontrolled price method would result in virtually the same transfer price.

It is possible that a transfer price determined by the general rule and an IRS-determined transfer price could be equal or nearly so for a profit/cost center if the contribution margin technique were used to maintain the profit concept. The contribution margin technique, however, was recommended as a means of expediently maintaining the motivation of a profit center by removing a potential source of low motivation, i.e., a product transferred at cost. Because the contribution margin technique results in an arbitrary profit split, it was recommended that when this technique is used, performance evaluation be based on cost analysis rather than profit analysis. Hence, while the IRS and the general rule may result in the same transfer price because both are using the contribution margin technique, the determination of taxes will be arbitrary.

In summary, although the general rule and IRS methods sometimes will result in the same transfer price, there is no reason why this always should be so. The determination of taxes is not always compatible with promoting profit maximization and enhancing performance evaluation, so separate transfer prices often will be necessary for the separate objectives of the IRS and the management control process.

Domestic International Sales Corporation (DISC)

Although domestic international sales corporations are not discussed in detail in this study, they are mentioned here because they are affected by Section 482 and have significant tax advantages.

The purpose of a DISC is to encourage U.S. manufacturers to increase exports by providing them with substantial tax benefits. The basic tax advantage is the deferral of federal income tax on a significant portion of the DISC's earnings. The benefit is enhanced by favorable transfer pricing rules that increase the amount of taxable income of the DISC.[17] The transfer pricing rules are quoted next.

> In the case of a sale of export property to a DISC by a person described in Section 482, the taxable income of such DISC and such person shall be based upon a transfer price which would allow such DISC to derive taxable income attributable to such sale (regardless of the sales price actually charged) in the amount which does not exceed the greatest of (1) 4% of the qualified export receipts on the sale of such property by the DISC plus 10% of the export promotion expenses of such DISC attributable to such receipts, (2) 50% of the combined taxable income of such DISC and such person which is attributable to the qualified export receipts on such property derived as the result of a sale by the DISC plus 10% of the export promotion expenses of such DISC attributable to such receipts, or (3) taxable income based upon the sales price actually charged (but subject to the rules provided in Section 482).[18]

When rules (1) or (2) are used, Section 482 does not apply. Under these rules, which are designed to simplify compliance, the transfer price from the related supplies to the DISC is computed only after the DISC sells the goods to a customer. The DISC and its supplier may make adjustments upward or downward following the close of the taxable year in which the DISC sells the goods in order to obtain the most favorable allocation of income permitted by these rules.

The favorable tax aspects and transfer pricing rules have made DISCs very popular.

Summary

There are a number of objectives involved in international transfer pricing besides fulfilling the objectives of the management control process. Often these objectives are so important that they override the objectives of the management control process, resulting in transfer prices that neither promote profit maximization nor enhance performance evaluation.

One of the most influential objectives is the minimization of income taxes, which is achieved by an allocation of profit among the countries involved in the manufacture and sale of the product. In the United States, the allocation of profit is regulated by Section 482 of the Internal Revenue Code. Section 482 specifies three methods of determining transfer prices: the comparable uncontrolled price method, the resale price method, and the cost-plus method. In addition, the Section allows the use of any other method that the taxpayer can show is more appropriate.

Although important, international transfer pricing and tax considerations are only a part of this research study. The primary focus has been on domestic transfer pricing. This study investigated the transfer pricing practices of 19 major companies to determine the types of transfer pricing techniques being used and the reasons why they were used. From this information and an analysis of the relationship of transfer pricing to the management control process, the general rule, TP = SVC + LCM, was developed and illustrated.

The general rule is a procedure for establishing the transfer price that will promote profit maximization while enhancing performance evaluation. The general rule is not a single transfer pricing technique; it is a rule that ties together a number of techniques. To use the general rule, a company first must determine the type of competitive market it faces. When this is determined, application of the general rule will lead the company to the appropriate transfer price and the type of responsibility center that can be used.

The purpose of this research study was to investigate the transfer pricing techniques of U.S.-based companies and to suggest guidelines for selecting transfer pricing techniques. It is hoped that fulfilling these objectives has been a step forward in understanding and solving some of the problems caused by transfer pricing.

Notes

1. This section is influenced by James S. Shulman, *Transfer Pricing in Multinational Business,* Soldiers Field Press, Massachusetts, 1975, pp. 18-33.
2. James S. Shulman, "When the Price Is Wrong—By Design," *Columbia Journal of World Business,* May-June 1967, pp. 69-76.
3. Duane Malmstrom, "Accommodating Exchange Rate Fluctuations in Intercompany Pricing and Invoicing," *Management Accounting,* September 1977, pp. 24-28. Malmstrom is an employee of Honeywell, Inc., one of the companies in this study.
4. A controlled sale is one between related parties. An uncontrolled sale is an arm's-length sale between unrelated parties. A controlled group is one of the related parties making an internal transfer of tangible property.
5. Reg. 1.482-2(e)(2)(ii).
6. The IRC uses the words "definite and reasonably ascertainable effect." The point at which a difference is no longer definite or reasonably ascertainable is likely to be difficult to determine and is the source of many taxpayer-IRS disputes. Reg. 1.482-2(e)(2)(ii).
7. Reg. 1.482-2(e)(2)(iii).
8. Reg. 1.482-2(e)(2)(iv).
9. Reg. 1.482-2(e)(3)(i).
10. Reg. 1.482-2(e)(3)(ii).
11. Reg. 1.482-2(e)(3)(vi).
12. Reg. 1.482-2(e)(4)(ii).
13. *Eli Lilly and Co. v. U.S.,* 372 F.2d 990 (Ct. Cl. 1967).
14. *Frank v. International Canadian Corp.,* 308 F.2d 520 (9th Cir. 1962).
15. Reg. 1.482-2(e)(1)(iii).
16. This list is based on T.M. 230-2rd, "Allocations (Sec. 482) — Specific Transactions," (Tax Management, Inc., 1978), p. A-35-37.
17. See Reg. 1.943-1 for a list of qualifications necessary to establish a DISC.
18. Reg. 1.944(a).

Appendix A

The Relationship Between the Management Control Process and Transfer Pricing

The management control process (MCP) has two major objectives. They are (1) to guide the members of the company toward the company's goals and (2) to evaluate the progress of the company's segments toward these goals. A general model of the MCP is shown in Exhibit A-1 (page 137). The model can be described as follows:

> The triangular performance center (1) represents some measurable and controllable characteristic in an operating system. It might refer to the quality or quantity of output, the efficiency of input utilization, employee morale, or an agreed upon method of striving for goal achievement. The second step (2) of the control process involves measuring the characteristic(s) in question. This could involve literal measurements with a micrometer or a subjective performance rating of a subordinate by a superior. The next step (3) involves comparing the actual results (as measured) with expected performance. Comparison suggests some explicit or, at least, implicit standards which can be used as a frame of reference. Steps (4), (5), and (6) show an elaboration of the decision-maker (effector) element of the control process. Several alternative courses of action are typically open, based on the results of the appraisal step. If there is no deviation or if performance exceeds expectation, there may be no adjustment to the system, and the process looks back to the performance center for a subsequent measurement. Above-standard performance, however, may lead to adjustment in aspiration level and hence call for an upward adjustment in standards.
>
> If a deviation is noted but a characteristic is uncontrollable, there would be no change in performance, standards, or plans. Another case might involve recognition of a deviation between actual and expected performance, but one which is not large enough to require a change to be effected.

Another possibility involves an acceptable deviation for the present, but recognition that some adjustment is necessary to keep the system "in control" in the future. Another alternative is a clearly unacceptable deviation which necessitates relatively immediate change in either the standards, procedures, or performance. Feedback in the latter two cases flows into the subsystem for setting standards (control plan) as well as to the major plan and corrective subplan for the performance center. Feedback may affect only the subsystem which includes the particular performance center, or, on the other hand, it may involve changes which also affect the master or comprehensive plan to which the control process relates.

Item (6) cuts across all the appraisal alternatives and relates to some sort of aggregate or overall control process which relies on cumulative information to be used as raw material for decision making. Certain aspects may have a rather high threshold before the control process evokes significant adjustments in the system.

Just as the elements cited previously refer to any control system, the process described herein applies to any control system regardless of the degree of sophistication in the various steps outlined. The means employed to sense, compare, and effect may be highly programmed, mechanistic, and computerized, or subjective human beings may be involved in each step of the process. The inclusion of human decision makers in the process tends to make the control system relatively more open.[1]

Although stated somewhat technically, the description of the management control process shows it is an elaborate process used for controlling a diversity of activities and elements within the organization.

Transfer pricing can be viewed as a system within the MCP. Viewed in this manner, transfer pricing involves more than simply determining the amount of the transfer price. The transfer pricing system within the MCP is shown in Exhibit A-1 and can be described as follows: After the major plan for the organization is developed, the organizational factors (1a) that can influence transfer pricing decisions (2a) are determined. The main factors are managerial, such as desire to use profit centers rather than cost centers, and environmental, such as tax considerations, the influences of a host country's government, or the type of market faced by a company. A consideration of these and other factors leads to a decision to use certain transfer pricing techniques (3a) in the organization. These transfer pricing techniques are communicated to the performance centers (1) for use in calculating actual transfer prices.

The controller's role in the transfer pricing system involves (1) providing input for the selection of the transfer pricing technique, (2) monitoring transfer pricing throughout the company, and (3) measuring the results of transfer pricing via reports on the performance of

EXHIBIT A-1

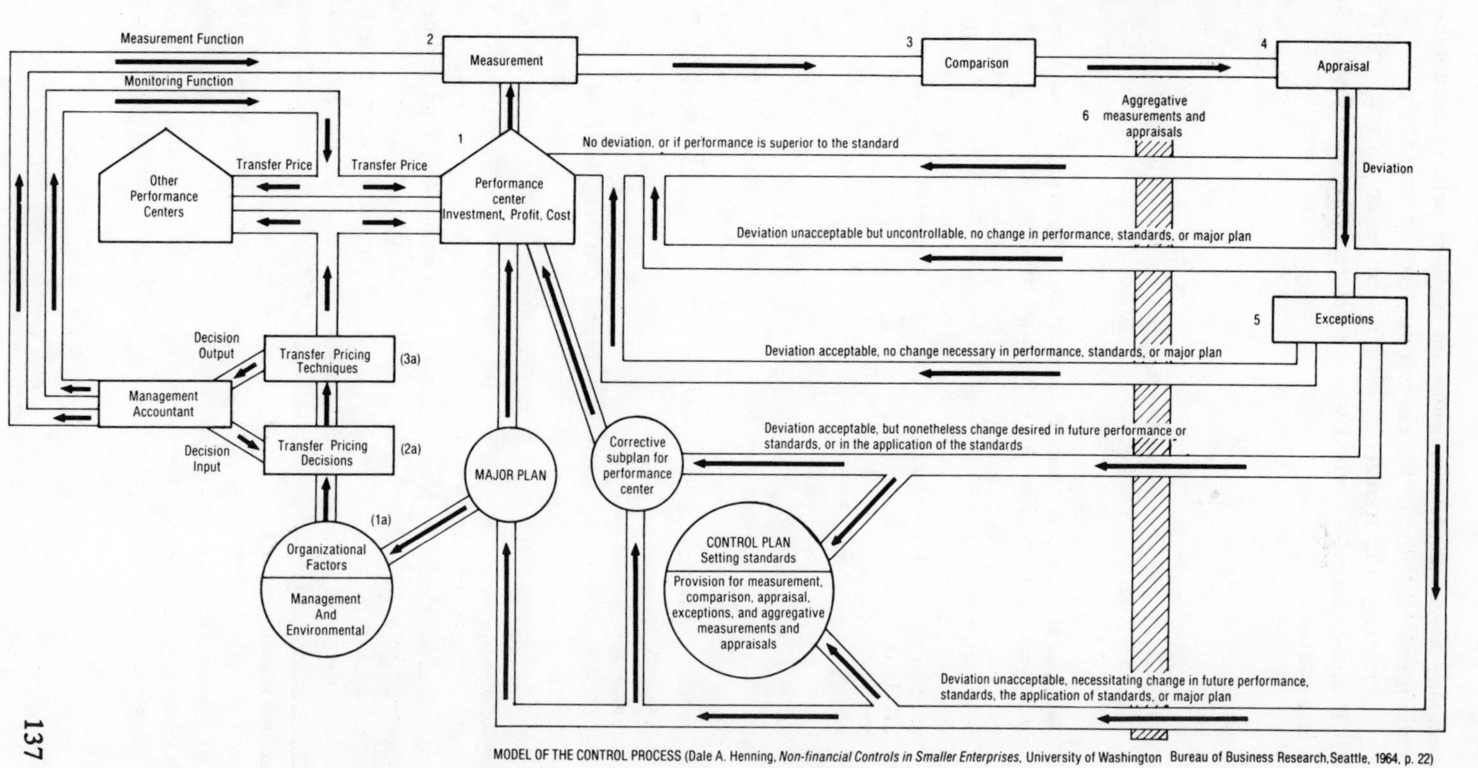

MODEL OF THE CONTROL PROCESS (Dale A. Henning, *Non-financial Controls in Smaller Enterprises*, University of Washington Bureau of Business Research, Seattle, 1964, p. 22)

company segments. His decisions on transfer pricing cannot be made without consideration of the major objectives of the MCP.

In summary, the transfer pricing system is an intricate part of the MCP and cannot be studied without reference to the broader process it is a part of.

Note

1. Fremont E. Kast and James E. Rosenzweig, *Organization and Management: a Systems Approach*, New York: McGraw-Hill Co., 1974, p. 471-473.

Appendix B

The Theory of Transfer Pricing

Contributions to the theory of transfer pricing have come primarily from microeconomics and secondarily from operations research and accounting. Many of these contributions are quite complicated and somewhat abstract. Nevertheless, the theoretical developments of transfer pricing are very important because they have had a significant impact on current views of transfer pricing. This appendix is a discussion of the more basic elements of one of the major contributions to transfer pricing theory.

Hirshleifer's Analysis

The principal contributor to the theory of transfer pricing is economist Jack Hirshleifer.[1] Although Hirshleifer's analysis has on many occasions been used as support for setting transfer prices at the marginal cost of the transferring division, a close review of Hirshleifer's analysis reveals that he believed marginal cost transfer prices to be appropriate only in special circumstances. An examination of Hirshleifer's analysis will show why this is so.

Hirshleifer wanted to show how a firm using transfer pricing between a manufacturing division and a distribution (selling) division could select the transfer price that would maximize the firm's profits. He begins his analysis with the least complex situation and moves to increasingly more complicated situations.

For the first analysis, assume that the manufacturing division can sell the units it produces only to the distribution division. The distribution division in turn sells the products to the market, which is assumed to be perfectly competitive; i.e., the firm can sell all the units it produces at the same price.[2] The object for the firm is to select a transfer price that will result in a level of production and sales for the manufacturing and distributing divisions that will maximize the firm's profit. This analysis is shown in Exhibit B-1.

EXHIBIT B-1

Best Joint Level of Output

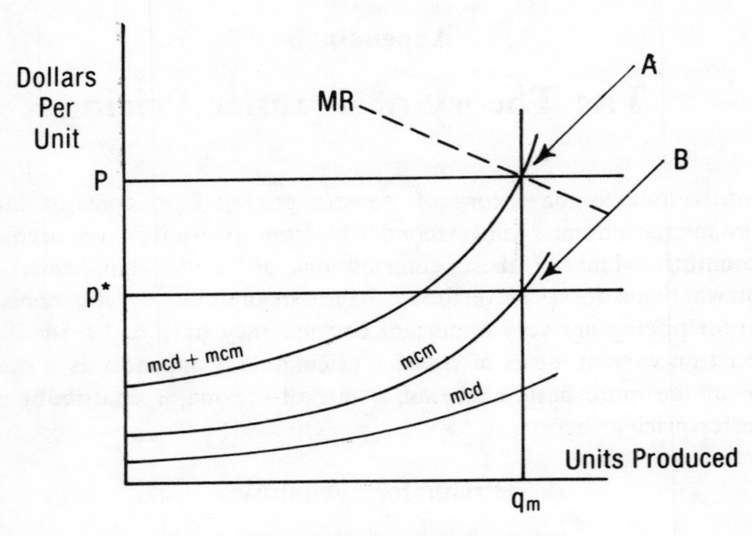

where mcm = marginal cost of manufacturing
mcd = marginal cost of distribution
P = marginal revenue with perfect competition
MR = marginal revenue with imperfect competition
q_m = optimal quantity of units to produce
p* = the transfer price

For the moment, ignore the line labeled MR. In order for the firm to maximize its total profits, it should expand production until the marginal cost of the next unit to be produced will equal or exceed the marginal revenue from the unit. In order to do this, the firm will (1) determine the marginal cost of manufacturing (mcm), (2) determine the marginal cost of distribution (mcd), and (3) add the marginal cost of distribution to the marginal cost of manufacturing (mcm + mcd).

The point (labeled A) at which mcm plus mcd intersects P (the marginal revenue) is the optimal level of output where profit maximization is achieved. A line is dropped straight down to the horizontal axis to determine that the optimal level of production is q_m.

Knowing that q_m is the optimal level of production will enable the firm to determine the transfer price. Notice that when the line was dropped straight down to the horizontal axis from $mcm + mcd = P$, it crossed mcm at Point B. If a straight line is drawn from Point B across to the vertical axis, the transfer price, p^*, is determined. Therefore, the firm establishes the transfer price and the quantity of units to produce which will maximize the firm's profits.

If the assumption of perfect competition for the final product is changed to imperfect competition, the analysis is essentially the same except that P no longer represents the marginal revenue of the firm. Instead, MR (the dashed line) represents the firm's marginal revenue. As can be seen in Exhibit B-1, changing the assumption of perfect competition for the final product has not changed the analysis. The transfer price, p^*, is still equal to the marginal cost of the manufacturing division (mcm) at q_m units produced.[3]

The next step in the analysis is to allow the manufacturing division to sell its output either internally to the distribution division or externally where the market for the manufacturing division's product is perfectly competitive. This analysis is shown in Exhibit B-2.

As before, ignore the dashed line for a moment. By doing so, it is assumed that the external market for the final product also is perfectly competitive; i.e., P equals the marginal revenue for the firm.

From the view of the firm, the object is still to maximize the total firm's profits, but now there are two ways of generating revenue. One is to sell the units produced by the manufacturing division to buyers outside the firm. The other is to sell the units produced by the manufacturing division to the distributing division, which, after further processing, sells them outside the firm.

Because there is an outside market for the manufacturing division's units with price, p, the number of units that should be produced by the manufacturing division is determined by the intersection of mcm and p at point A. Dropping a line straight down from point A to the horizontal axis gives q_m units to be produced by the manufacturing division, a production level which will result in the maximum profit for the division.

The distribution division either could buy the units it needs from the manufacturing division at price, p, or from a competitor of the manufacturing division at the same price. Therefore, to maximize the distribution division's profit, mcd should be added to p. This determines the firm's marginal cost (MC). The point at which p plus mcd equals P (point B) determines the optimal quantity for the distribution division

EXHIBIT B-2

Perfectly Competitive Market for Intermediate Product

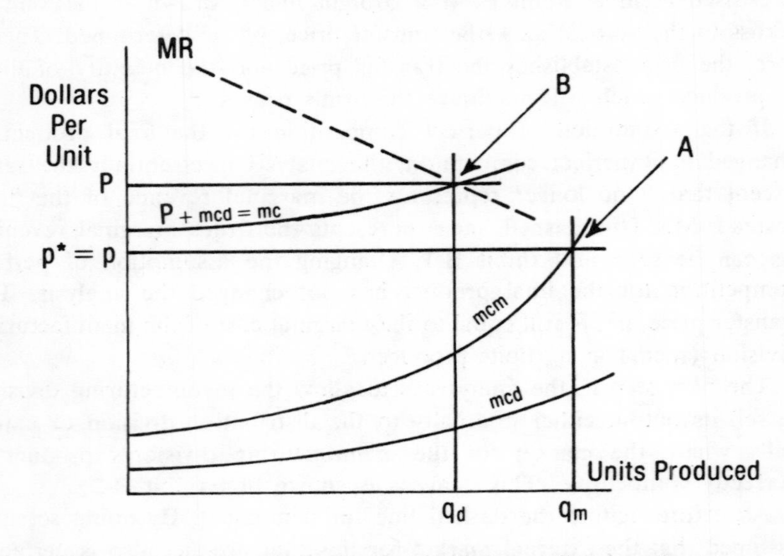

where p = the market price for the intermediate product (the marginal revenue (MR) for the manufacturing division).

where q_d = Optimal number of units for the distribution division to purchase.

---

to buy from the manufacturing division or a competitor for further processing. This entire procedure also leads to the maximum profit for the firm, so the transfer price, p^*, is set equal to p.

When the market for the final product is not perfectly competitive, the analysis is the same. Substitute MR (the dashed line) for P.[4] The optimal quantity for the distributing division is still q_d at $p + mcd = MR$. Therefore, the transfer price, p^*, is determined by equating the marginal cost of the manufacturing division (mcm) to the market prices of the intermediate product, p, which is also the marginal revenue curve for the manufacturing division.

The analysis is more complicated if the assumption of perfect competition for the products sold by the manufacturing division is dropped. The analysis for an imperfect market for the intermediate market and an imperfect market for the final product is shown in Exhibit B-3.

EXHIBIT B-3

Imperfectly Competitive Markets for the Intermediate and Final Product

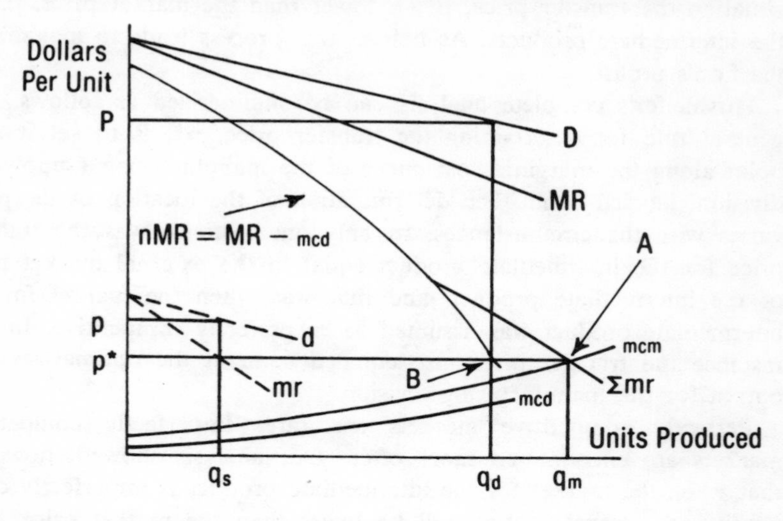

where D = demand for the final product

d = external demand for the intermediate product

Σmr = nMR + mr

nMR = the market marginal revenue curve for the final product less the marginal distribution cost curve (nMR = MR − mcd), referred to as the net marginal revenue

The optimal transfer price is found analytically by a price discrimination technique. The point at which mcm and Σmr intersect, Point A, determines both the optimal quantity for the manufacturing division to produce, q_m, and the transfer price, p*. At Point A, the marginal revenue (Σmr) and marginal cost (mcm) of the manufacturing division are equal. The line Σmr is the sum of line nMR, which is the net marginal revenue for products sold externally by the distribution division, and mr, which is the marginal revenue for products sold externally by the manufacturing division.

The number of units purchased by the distribution division, q_d, is determined at Point B, where nMR intersects the line drawn from Point A to the vertical axis. The number of units sold outside the firm by the manufacturing division is q_m minus q_d equals q_s. The price of the q_s sold outside the firm is determined by following the q_s line up to d and across to the vertical axis at price, p. Notice that in this situation the transfer price, p*, is lower than the market price, p, for the intermediate products. As before, this process leads to maximizing the firm's profits.

Hirshleifer's complete analysis can be summarized as follows. The general rule for determining the transfer price, p*, is to set it at a point along the marginal cost curve of the manufacturing (supplying) division, labeled mcm. The determination of the location of the point varies with the circumstances. In only one instance was the transfer price for the intermediate product equal to the external market price of the intermediate product, and that was when the market for the intermediate product was assumed to be perfectly competitive. In that instance the transfer price also equaled mcm at the optimal level of output for the manufacturing division.

Perfectly competitive markets are rare. Imperfectly competitive markets are encountered more often. Our analysis showed, however, that when the market for the intermediate product is imperfectly competitive, the transfer price will be lower than the market price. Had the transfer price been set at the market price, the manufacturing division would have oversupplied and the distribution division would have underpurchased, leading to less than optimal firm profits.

Is Marginal Cost the Best Transfer Pricing Technique?

It would seem from Hirshleifer's analysis that marginal cost transfer pricing is the best for all firms since it is consistent with maximization of the firm's profits. Hirshleifer's general rule, however, is based on two assumptions not yet discussed: cost independence[5] and demand independence.

Cost independence means that the operating costs of each division are independent of the level of operations being carried on by other divisions. An example of cost independence is a chain of retail stores, such as Sears, Roebuck and Co. Each store is really selling local retailing services. The marginal cost of business for each store is substantially independent of the costs of the other stores except for certain supply operations handled on a central basis and affected by the level of retail sales in each store.

Demand independence means that an additional external sale by either division does not reduce the external demand for the product of the other division. An example of demand independence would be a firm producing copper from ore; the firm transfers copper internally for use in making copper wire but sells copper externally for use in making pots and pans.

Practically speaking, there is a very low probability that *both* cost independence and demand independence will exist simultaneously for any one firm. If demand dependence exists and the market for the intermediate product is imperfectly competitive (the more frequent case), the correct transfer price exists somewhere between mcm and the market price for the intermediate product, p. If cost dependence exists, the analysis, according to Hirshleifer, is so complex that the correct transfer price cannot be determined. Naturally, then, with a low probability that both demand and cost independence will exist simultaneously, there is very little likelihood that Hirshleifer's rule of setting the transfer price at mcm is useful.

Even when marginal cost transfer prices are appropriate, special rules and procedures will be needed to avoid the possibility that the supplying or receiving division will act as a monopoly with respect to the other. If one division can exploit a monopoly position, the transfer price established will not be the marginal cost of the supplying division.[6] The only practical means of avoiding this situation would be for a higher level in the firm to establish the transfer prices for the divisions. When this occurs, however, the divisions surrender a considerable degree of their autonomy; this procedure is therefore counter to the reasons for establishing divisions as profit centers.

Hirshleifer's analysis has been extended by Gould[7] to take into consideration those circumstances where there may be costs associated with using an external market. Gould's analysis also depends on the assumptions of cost and demand independence, but, while conceptually elegant, has not answered the question of what transfer pricing technique to use and when to use it. Gould does bring out some very interesting points about transfer pricing that pertain to this monograph.

> In general, when divisions are judged on their profits and at the same time have a hand in determining transfer prices, there is both the incentive and opportunity to cheat. How serious a view one takes on these difficulties depends on what one conceives to be the major functions of transfer pricing. Broadly speaking there are two schools of thought. The first places most emphasis on the value of judging divisional performance by profit figures and the consequent stimulus to managers. If this view is held, it may be thought that the increase in managerial efficiency far outweighs the losses that are likely to arise from nonoptimal outputs consequent on monopolistic "extortion" by the divisions.

The second school attaches major importance to the savings in the costs of transmitting and processing information which simulation of the price mechanism within the firm can bring. Holders of this view might be quite happy to abandon incentives related to conventional divisional profit and loss accounts, merely instructing divisional managers to equate MC (or NMR) with the transfer price.[8]

The two views above might be labeled the school of transfer pricing for performance evaluation and the school of transfer pricing for profit maximization. This research study has taken a compromise position by emphasizing both criteria of performance evaluation and profit maximization in determining the correct transfer price. Thus, this monograph represents a pragmatic compromise between the two schools.

Notes

1. Jack Hirshleifer, "On the Economics of Transfer Pricing," *Journal of Business,* July 1956, pp. 172-184; "Economics of the Divisionalized Firm," *Journal of Business,* April 1957, pp. 96-108 and "Internal Pricing and Decentralized Decisions" in *Management Controls: New Directions in Basic Research,* ed. Bonini, Jaedicke and Wagner, New York: McGraw-Hill, Inc., 1964, pp. 418-429.
2. Perfect competition occurs when no single producer of a product is large enough to influence the market price of that product by expanding or restricting production. In the U.S. economy, perfect competition is not found often.
3. In Exhibit B-1, lines MR and P were made to deliberately cross line mcm + mcd at the same point as a matter of convenience rather than necessity in the analysis.
4. In Exhibit B-2, lines MR and P were made to deliberately cross line MC (p + mcd) at the same point as a matter of convenience rather than necessity in the analysis.
5. In his early articles, Hirshleifer referred to a similar independence as technocogical independence. Cost independence has wider applicability.
6. Hirshleifer, *op cit.*
7. J. R. Gould, "Internal Pricing in Firms When There Are Costs of Using an Outside Market," *Journal of Business* (January 1964), pp. 61-7.
8. Ibid. p. 66.

Bibliography

Abdel-khalik, A. Rashad and Edward J. Lusk, "Transfer Pricing — A Synthesis," *The Accounting Review.* 49 (January 1974): 8-23.

Abdel-khalik, A. Rashad and Edward J. Lusk, "Transfer Pricing — A Synthesis: A Reply," *The Accounting Review.* 50 (April 1975): 355-358.

Bailey, Andrew D. Jr., and Warren Boe Jr., "Goal and Resource Transfers in the Multigoal Organization," *The Accounting Review.* 51 (July 1976): 559-73.

Barrett, M. Edgar, "Case of the Tangled Transfer Price," *Harvard Business Review.* 55 (May 1977): 20-2, 26, 28, 32, 36, 176, 178.

Benston, George J. *Contemporary Cost Accounting and Control.* 2nd ed. Encino, Calif.: Dickenson Publishing Co., 1977.

Bierman, Harold, Jr., and Thomas R. Dyckman. *Managerial Cost Accounting.* New York: Macmillan Publishing Co., Inc., 1976.

Burton, R.M., W.W. Damon and D.W. Loughridge. "Economics of Decomposition: Resource Allocation vs. Transfer Pricing," *Decision Sciences.* 5 (July 1974): 297-310.

Carey, George. "How to Handle Pricing Situations not Covered in the Proposed DISC Regulations," *Journal of Taxation.* 41 (September 1974): 197-81.

Chandra, Gyan. "Divisional Performance and Transfer Pricing," *Management Accountant.* 8 (December 1973): 818-24.

Choi, Frederick R.W. "Multinational Challenges for Managerial Accountants," *Journal of Contemporary Business.* 4 (Autumn 1975): 51-67.

Clay, Michael. "Contribution Theory in Practice," *The Accountant.* 169 (August 9, 1973): 183-6.

Clinton, G.S. "Ditton Corvedale Company," *Management Accounting.* 56 (February 1978): 69-70.

Cowen, S.S. "Multinational Transfer Pricing," *Management Accounting.* 60 (January 1979): 17-22.

Crompton, Walter H. "Transfer Pricing: A Proposal," *Management Accounting*. 53 (April 1972): 46-8.

Dagher, Samir P. "What's the Price When a Company Buys from Itself?" *Administrative Management*. 37 (May 1977): 32-4.

Dale, E. *Planning and Developing the Company Organization Structure*. New York: American Management Association, 1952.

Dascher, Paul E. "Transfer Pricing — Some Behavioral Observations," *Managerial Planning*. 21 (November/December 1972): 17-21.

Dittman, David A. "Transfer Pricing and Decentralization," *Management Accounting*. 54 (November 1972): 47-50.

Dittman, David A. and Kenneth R. Ferris. "Profit Centre: A Satisfaction Generating Concept," *Accounting and Business Research*. 8 (Autumn 1978): 242-5.

Edwards, James Don and Roger A. Roemmich. "Transfer Pricing: The Wrong Tool for Performance Evaluation," *Cost and Management*. 50 (January-February 1976): 35-37.

Emmanuel, C.R. "Birch Paper Company: A Possible Solution to the Interdivisional Pricing Problem," *Accountant's Magazine*. 81 (May 1977): 196-8.

Emmanuel, Clive. "Transfer Pricing: A Diagnosis and Possible Solution to Dysfunctional Decision-Making in the Divisionalised Company," *Management International Review*. 17 (1977): 45-59.

Fantl, I.L. "Transfer Pricing — Tread Carefully," *CPA Journal*. 44 (December 1974): 42-6.

Ferrara, William L. "Accounting for Performance Evaluation and Decision-Making," *Management Accounting*. 58 (December 1976): 13-19.

Flavell, R.B. "Divisionalization and Transfer Pricing: A Review," *Omega*. 5 (1977): 543-56.

The Friedlander Corporation v. Commissioner, 25 TC 70.

Fuller, J.P. "Service Asserts Civil Fraud in Section 482 Intercompany Pricing Decision," *The Journal of Taxation*. 45 (November 1976): 282-5.

Galbraith, J.R. "Organization Design: An Information Processing View," In *Organizational Planning: Cases and Concepts*, pp. 49-74. Edited by J.W. Lorsh and P.R. Lawrence. Georgetown, Ontario: Irwin-Dorsey Limited, 1972.

Gibson, James L., John M. Ivancevich and James H. Donnelly Jr. *Organizations: Structure, Process, Behavior*. Dallas, Tex.: Business Publications, Inc., 1973.

Goetz, Billy E. "Transfer Prices: An Exercise in Relevancy and Goal Congruence," *The Accounting Review*. 42 (July 1967): 435-40.

Gould, J.R. "Internal Pricing in Firms When There Are Costs of Using an Outside Market," *Journal of Business*. 37 (January 1964): 61-67.

Granick, David. "National Differences in the Use of Internal Transfer Prices," *California Management Review*. 17 (Summer 1975): 28-40.

Hirshleifer, Jack. "Economics of the Divisionalized Firm," *The Journal of Business* 16 (April 1957): 96-108.

Hirshleifer, Jack. "Internal Pricing and Decentralized Decisions," In *Management Controls: New Directions in Basic Research,* pp. 418-29. Edited by Bonini, Jaedicke, and Wagner, New York: McGraw Hill, Inc., 1964.

Hirshleifer, Jack. "On the Economics of Transfer Pricing," *The Journal of Business*. 16 (July 1956): 172-184.

Horngren, Charles. "A Contribution Margin Approach to the Analysis of Capacity Utilization," *The Accounting Review*. 42 (April 1967): 254-64.

Horngren, Charles. *Cost Accounting: A Managerial Emphasis,* Englewood Cliffs, N.J.: Prentice-Hall, Inc., 1977.

Kalish, Richard H. "Intercompany Pricing: How to Handle an International Tax Examination," *Tax Adviser*. 9 (April 1978): 196-205.

Kast, Fremont E. and James E. Rosenzweig. *Organization and Management: a Systems Approach*. New York: McGraw-Hill, Inc., 1974.

Lamp, Walter. "Multinational Whipping Boy," *Financial Executive*. 44 (December 1976): 44-6.

Langrana, Dinjar F. "Transfer Pricing: A Situational Approach," *Chartered Accountant*. 26 (September 1977): 163-6.

Larson, Raymond L. "Decentralization in Real Life," *Management Accounting*. 55 (March 1974): 28-32.

Lawrence, Paul R. and Jay W. Lorsch. "Differentiation and Integration in Complex Organizations," *Administrative Science Quarterly*. 12 (June 1967): 1-47.

Lawrence, P.R. and J.W. Lorsch. *Organization and Environment*. New York: Richard D. Irwin, 1967.

Liao, Shu S. "Responsibility Centers," *The CPA Journal*. 43 (October 1973): 897-901.

Lucien, K. "Transfer Pricing for the Cost of Funds in a Commercial Bank," *Management Accounting*. 60 (January 1979): 23-4.

Luthans, Fred. *Organizational Behavior*. New York: McGraw-Hill, Inc., 1973.

Macnair, H.S.A. "Transfer Pricing and Tax," *The Accountant*. 171 (August 1, 1974): 144-5.

Madison, R.L. "Responsibility Accounting and Transfer Pricing: Approach with Caution," *Management Accounting*. 60 (January 1979): 25-9.

Mailandt, Peter. "An Alternative to Transfer Pricing," *Business Horizons*. 17 (October 1975): 81-6.

Malmstrom, Duane. "Accommodating Exchange Rate Fluctuations in Intercompany Pricing and Invoicing," *Management Accounting*. 59 (September 1977): 24-8.

Mautz, R.D. *Financial Reporting by Diversified Companies*. New York: Financial Executives Research Foundation, 1968.

McNally, Graeme M. "Profit Centres and Transfer Prices — Are They Necessary?" *Accounting and Business Research*. 4 (Winter 1973): 13-22.

Merville, L.J. and J.W. Petty. "Transfer Pricing for the Multinational Firm," *Accounting Review*. 53 (October 1978): 935-51.

Milburn, J. Alex. "International Transfer Transaction: What Price?" *CA Magazine*. 109 (December 1976): 22-7.

Morris, James R. "Application of the Decomposition Principle to Financial Decision Models," *Journal of Financial and Quantitative Analysis*. 10 (March 1975): 37-65.

Mueller, Gerhard G. "Accounting for Multinationals," *Accountancy*. 86 (July 1975): 68-75.

Nagy, Richard J. "Transfer Price Accounting for MNCs," *Management Accounting*. 59 (January 1978): 34-8.

National Association of Cost Accountants. *Accounting for Intracompany Transfers*. Research Series No. 30. New York: National Association of Cost Accountants, 1956.

National Industrial Conference Board. *Interdivisional Transfer Pricing*. Business Policy Study No. 122. New York: National Industrial Conference Board, 1967.

Newman, William H., Charles E. Summer and E. Kirby Warren. *The Process of Management — Concepts, Behavior, and Practice*. 3rd ed. Englewood Cliffs, N.J.: Prentice-Hall, Inc., 1972.

"Numbers Game: Who's Shafting Whom?" *Forbes*. (January 15, 1976): 38-39.

Onsi, Mohamed. "A Transfer Pricing System Based on Opportunity Cost," *The Accounting Review*. 45 (July 1970): 535-543.

Onsi, Mohamed. "Transfer Pricing System Based on Opportunity Costs: a Reply," *Accounting Review*. 49 (January 1974): 129-31.

Rahl, James A. "Overview of the Direction of U.S. Antitrust Law — Problems of the Multinational — 2," *Toward a National Antitrust Policy*. New York: National Industrial Conference Board, 1976, pp. 81-8.

Ricks, David A. and Larry E. Tischer. "Multinational Corporate Financial Control Systems: Problems and Recommendations," *Akron Business and Economic Review*. 5 (Spring 1974): 20-5.

Ronen, J. "Transfer Pricing — A Synthesis: A Comment," *Accounting Review*. 50 (April 1975): 351-4.

Ronen, Joshua and George McKinney, III. "Transfer Pricing for Divisional Autonomy," *Journal of Accounting Research*. 8 (Spring 1970): 99-112.

Ross-Skinner, Jean. "Multinational vs. the Tax Collector," *Duns Review*. (February 1976): 68-69.

Schiff, Michael. "A Note on Transfer Pricing and Industry Segment Reporting," *Journal of Accounting, Auditing & Finance*. 2 (Spring 1979): 224-31.

Schwab, Richard J. "Contribution Approach to Transfer Pricing," *Management Accounting*. 56 (February 1975): 46-8.

Sharaw, Itzhak. "Transfer Pricing — Diversity of Goals and Practices," *Journal of Accountancy*. 137 (April 1974): 56-62.

Shaub, H. James. "Transfer Pricing in a Decentralized Organization," *Management Accounting*. 59 (April 1978): 33-6, 42.

Solomons, David. *Divisional Performance: Measurement and Control*. New York: Financial Executives Research Foundation, 1965.

Shulman, James S. *Transfer Pricing in Multinational Business*. Boston: Soldiers Field Press, 1975.

Shulman, James. "When the Price is Wrong — By Design," *Columbia Journal of World Business*. 2 (May-June 1967): 69-76.

Stone, Willard E. "Legal Implications of Intracompany Pricing," *The Accounting Review*. 39 (January 1964): 38-42.

Sutherland, Timothy F. *Measuring Performance Within the Refining and Marketing Segments of the United States Energy Industry: An Appraisal of the Need for Developing Estimates of Functional Profitability*. Washington, D.C.: R. Shriver Associates, 1978.

Talwar, Akshey K. "Transfer Pricing System Based on Opportunity Costs: A Comment," *Accounting Review*. 49 (January 1974) 126-8.

Tang, Roger Y., C. K. Walter and Robert H. Raymond. "Transfer Pricing — Japanese vs. American Style," *Management Accounting*. 60 (January 1979): 12-16.

Tax Management, Inc. "Allocations (Sec. 482) — Specific Transactions," *T.M. 230-2nd*. Tax Management, Inc., 1978, A-35-37.

Tewes, James A. "Valuing Bank Funds for Allocation and Pricing Decisions," *Managing Accounting*. 58 (November 1976): 27-33.

"Transfer Pricing: Fiddlers Beware," *Economist*. 269 (November 11, 1978): 113.

Troxel, Richard B. "On Transfer Pricing," *The CPA Journal*. 43 (October 1973): 895-7.

26 U.S.C., Sec. 482 (1954) and 26 C.F.R. 1,482.

United States Steel Corporation v. Commissioner, TC Memo 1977-140.

Vendig, Richard E. "A Three-Part Transfer Price," *Management Accounting*. 55 (September 1973): 33-6.

Watson, David J.H. and John V. Baumler, "Transfer Pricing: A Behavioral Context," *Accounting Review*. 50 (July 1975): 466-74.

Young, Alex. "Birch Paper Company: A Transfer Pricing Case Study," *Accountant's Magazine*. 80 (August 1976): 308-11.

National Association of Accountants Committee on Research 1979-1980

Calvin A. Vobroucek
Chairman
Caterpillar Tractor Company
Peoria, Ill.

George Bannon
Bethlehem Steel Corp.
Bethlehem, Pa.

Richard F. Bebee
Alexander Grant & Co.
Chicago, Ill.

Robert U. Boehman
Paoli Chair Company, Inc.
Paoli, Ind.

Germain Böer
Vanderbilt University
Nashville, Tenn.

Henry L. Clayton Sr.
Corning Glass Works
Corning, N.Y.

Paul E. Dascher
Drexel University
Philadelphia, Pa.

Dwight H. Davis
A. O. Smith Corp.
Kankakee, Ill.

Paul H. Davis
Solar Turbines International
San Diego, Calif.

Geraldine F. Dominiak
Texas Christian University
Ft. Worth, Tex.

Patricia P. Douglas
University of Montana
Missoula, Mont.

J. Bernard Eck
May, Zima & Co.
Daytona Beach, Fla.

Homer R. Figler
Ernst & Whinney
New York, N.Y.

Charles L. Grant
Becton Dickinson & Co.
East Rutherford, N.J.

John L. Hanson
Electro Corporation
Sarasota, Fla.

Glen R. Kellam
The Upjohn Company
Kalamazoo, Mich.

Donald A. Key
Ernst & Whinney
Dallas, Tex.

Henry M. Klein
Chrysler Corporation
Huntsville, Ala.

Carl M. Koontz
ALCOA
Alcoa, Tenn.

Paul H. Levine
Magnetic Analysis Corp.
Mt. Vernon, N.Y.

Joseph J. McCann
Ryan Homes Inc.
Pittsburgh, Pa.

Jack E. Meadows
Combustion Engineering, Inc.
Chattanooga, Tenn.

Ronald J. Patten
University of Connecticut
Storrs, Conn.

Howard O. Rockness
University of North Carolina
Chapel Hill, N.C.

W. Peter Salzarulo
Miami University
Oxford, Ohio

Henry A. Schwartz
IBM Corporation
Armonk, N.Y.

Milton F. Usry
Oklahoma State University
Stillwater, Okla.

Theodore N. Vaughn
Steelcase, Inc.
Grand Rapids, Mich.